DIVE

BAR

Dan Jones

DIVE BAR

OVER 50 COCKTAILS TO DRINK AFTER DARK

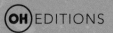

WHAT IS A DIVE BAR? 07
DIVE BAR RULES 08
KARAOKE PLAYLIST 10
DIVE SNACKS 12

THE DIVE BAR AT HOME 14
GLASSWARE 18
THE KNACK 22
THE BACK BAR 25

DIVE Bar

PROFILES

STONEWALL INN, NEW YORK, USA 28

CHEZ JEANNETTE, PARIS, FRANCE 41

B.Y.G, TOKYO, JAPAN 54

SALTY DAWG SALOON, ALASKA, USA 66

SUNNY'S, REDHOOK, USA 74

TRISHA'S, LONDON, UK 89

THE BEARDED TIT, REDFERN, AUSTRALIA 103

TWO SCHMUCKS, BARCELONA, SPAIN 126

CANDLELIGHT LOUNGE, NEW ORLEANS, USA 136

LA PIOJERA, SANTIAGO, CHILE 148

50
Classic Cocktail
RECIPES

1.	FERRARI	30
2.	AMERICANO	32
3.	NEGRONI	35
4.	NEGRONI BIANCO	36
5.	LONG ISLAND ICED TEA	38
6.	COSMOPOLITAN	43
7.	THE PERFECT GIN & TONIC	44
8.	BOILERMAKER	47
9.	MOSCOW MULE	48
10.	MANHATTAN	50
11.	BLOODY MARY	52
12.	BLOODY MARIA & HER SISTERS	56
13.	DAIQUIRI	59
14.	CUBA LIBRE	60
15.	GREYHOUND	63
16.	MARGARITA	64
17.	FRENCH 75	69
18.	GIMLET	70
19.	TOM COLLINS	72
20.	MARTINEZ	76
21.	WHISKY SOUR	78
22.	BOULEVARDIER	80
23.	VERMOUTH & TONIC	82
24.	ESPRESSO MARTINI	85
25.	DIRTY MARTINI	86
26.	PORN STAR MARTINI	90
27.	JÄGERBOMB	92
28.	MAN ABOUT TOWN	94
29.	NYC SOUR	96
30.	HOT APPLE CIDER	98
31.	GLÖGG	100
32.	MICHELADA	104
33.	SHANDY	107
34.	YALE COCKTAIL	108
35.	ROB ROY	111
36.	OYSTER BAY	113
37.	7 & 7	114
38.	LA LOUISIANE	116
39.	GIN, GRAPEFRUIT & BITTERS	118
40.	AMARETTO SOUR	120
41.	PINK GIN & TONIC	123
42.	COLD BREW SPRITZER	125
43.	OLD PAL	128
44.	NEGRONI SBAGLIATO	130
45.	SALTY DOG	132
46.	TEQUILA SUNRISE	134
47.	PALOMA	139
48.	ACAPULCO	140
49.	LAGERITA	143
50.	KAMIKAZE	144
51.	BARTENDER'S CHOICE	146
	INDEX	153
	ABOUT DAN JONES	158

WHAT IS A DIVE BAR?

What is a dive bar? And how might you know you are in one? Imagine it's late and you've hastily stumbled into the nearest bar with an open sign. You get a spot at the bar, pick your poison, and as you first raise a glass to your lips, you take a proper glance at the interior. There might be a comforting sense of shabbiness. A flicker of almost-dead neon. The aroma of stale pretzels. Halloween decorations still up in July. Perhaps there is an eclectic, junk-filled back bar and a plushie Garfield stuck to the register. Wood-effect tables. Duct-taped warm leatherette. A jukebox cranking out Brandy and Monica's 'The Boy is Mine'. And you think to yourself, 'Wait . . . am I in a dive?'

Perhaps we could identify a true dive bar not just by its interior décor, but by who we see around us, be it a three-legged dog on wheels, perhaps, or Sister Mary Clarence having a quiet Old Fashioned in the corner, or a drinker who gathers up their grocery bags at closing time, clearly having been there six hours too long.

Or should we look to the movies to discern the ultimate dive? There's the brash saloon in *Coyote Ugly* (2000) or The Imperial in Sydney, the drag bar on the wrong side of the tracks in *Priscilla, Queen of the Desert* (1994). Are English working men's clubs de facto dive bars? What about Australia's raucous RSLs (Returned and Services League)? They certainly both peddle delicious beige food and have lurid, optical-illusion carpets.

But perhaps what makes a bar a true dive is the atmosphere, as nebulous and ever-changing as a cloud of vape smoke; it's a feeling. You take another sip and then, like a ghostly voice from some distant spiritual plane, Natasha Bedingfield's 2004 mega-hit 'Unwritten' bursts forth from the juke box as every single dive drinker erupts with the same inspiring words: 'Today is where your book begins / The rest is still unwritten.' Now that's a dive bar.

DIVE BAR RULES

KEEP PHONE CALLS *to a* **MINIMUM**

NO EX-TEXTING
NO CRYING
NO SNARK

READ THE ROOM

IF CALLED UPON, YOU MUST SING KARAOKE

NO DOGS
(unless very cute)

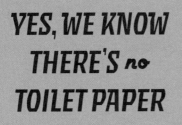

YES, WE KNOW THERE'S *no* TOILET PAPER

BE COURTEOUS!

TIP YOUR

BARTENDER, WAIT STAFF, DRAG QUEEN

BUY A STRANGER A DRINK *sometimes*

SHIRTS OPTIONAL, BUT NO BARE FEET

KARAOKE

PLAYLIST

ALL THE HITS, CLASSIC *and* MORE!

If your dive bar has karaoke – and if there is any good in the world, it does – it is essential you pre-prepare your favourite crowd-pleaser. We never know when we will be called upon to lift the spirits of those around us, and in those moments, we absolutely must turn toward the light.

MEMORISE *any of* **THE TRACKS BELOW, PERHAPS WITH SOME SIMPLE** *but* **DARING DANCE MOVES** *and,* **PLEASE, BE READY.**

#		#	
THE BOY IS MINE BRANDY AND MONICA	1	11	**WHEN YOU'RE GONE** BRYAN ADAMS AND MEL C
BABY, I'M BURNING DOLLY PARTON	2	12	**UMBRELLA** RIHANNA, FT. JAY-Z
KILLING IN THE NAME RAGE AGAINST THE MACHINE	3	13	**THAT DON'T IMPRESS ME MUCH** SHANIA TWAIN
EVERYBODY (BACKSTREET'S BACK) BACKSTREET BOYS	4	14	**PURE SHORES** ALL SAINTS
BENNIE & THE JETS ELTON JOHN	5	15	**SAY MY NAME** DESTINY'S CHILD
UNWRITTEN NATASHA BEDINGFIELD	6	16	**HOW WILL I KNOW** WHITNEY
SINGLE LADIES BEYONCÉ	7	17	**LEAVE (GET OUT)** JOJO
DON'T TELL ME MADONNA	8	18	**OOPS . . . I DID IT AGAIN** BRITNEY SPEARS
A THOUSAND MILES VANESSA CARLTON	9	19	**SINCE U BEEN GONE** KELLY CLARKSON
CALL ME MAYBE CARLY RAE JEPSEN	10	20	**TORN** NATALIE IMBRUGLIA

DIVE SNACKS

A PICTORIAL CELEBRATION *of the* DIVE BAR'S DIRTIEST SNACKS

-- SNACKS --

POPCORN .... CUTE LITTLE AIR-BASED NOTHINGS

PRETZELS .... DEATHLY SALTY

PEANUTS .... PERFECTLY GREASY

PORK SCRATCHINGS .... THE HAIRY ONES

POTATO CHIPS .... CONFIDENTLY SIMPLE

-- SMALL BITES --

PICKLED EGGS .... A FOOD CRIME

CHEESE CUBES .. HOW LONG HAVE THOSE BEEN SAT THERE?

PICKLES .... THE PERFECT – IF NOT TOO WET – SNACK

PICKLED ONIONS .... WHEN YOU KNOW YOU'RE NOT GOING TO GET A KISS

SCOTCH EGGS .... THE DIRTIEST DIVE SNACK

-- LARGE BITES --

PIZZA .... PERFECT IN EVERY WAY

SAUSAGE ROLLS .... DIRTY AND DELICIOUS KETCHUP OR MUSTARD?

SCAMPI FRIES .... THE BRITISH FISHY CORN SNACK

THE DIVE BAR at HOME

Turn down the lights, turn up the Céline Dion remix playlist,
pour the cheddar goldfish into bowls and pop your frozen tamales
in the microwave: it's time to recreate the dive bar at home.
You'll need some essential equipment, the right glassware,
an insane amount of booze, an abundance of beige snacks
and a truckload of ice.

THE TOOL BOX

Everything you need to master your own dive bar cocktail kit.

JIGGER

The standard shot measure for spirits and liqueurs around the world, having a jigger or two is essential. Available in different sizes, some with helpful half-measures, heavy metal jiggers are perfect, as are cocktail shaker caps, but plastic or glass versions are also acceptable . . . or even the single shot glass as a last-minute stand-in.

SHAKER

This is your single most important piece of kit, as very few spirit and citrus cocktails are possible without one. The classic metal shaker has three main parts: a base (known as the 'can'), a tight-fitting funnel top with built-in strainer and a small cap (which can also be used as a jigger). It's brilliantly straightforward. If you can't get your hands on one, empty out your pickle jar and improvise.

BLENDER

It's best to use crushed ice in blender cocktails, rather than starting with oversized cubes or rocks. Add your ice and/or frozen ingredients first, then the liquids and any other solids, and pulse gently before turning it up to the max. No need to strain. Once the consistency is smooth, pour into a glass and serve.

BAR
SPOON

The long, twisted bar spoon designed for stirring and, um, dribbling: the twisted stem allows for a slow pour to create ombré-toned drinks like the NYC Sour.

MIXING
GLASS

100% pure spirit recipes will usually need stirring with ice in a mixing glass rather than shaking; this is to limit dilution, ice chips and drama. The glass can be anything from a tough-ass straight-sided Boston to a straight-sided pint glass. A mixing glass can also allow for extra volume when attached to the can of your shaker. The two halves are locked together and you shake until the drink is chilled; a cocktail (Hawthorne) strainer can then be used to strain the drink into a fresh glass.

COCKTAIL
STRAINER

For when your shaker's built-in version isn't up to the job: the cocktail strainer – sometimes called a Hawthorne strainer – is a flat piece of kit trimmed with a spring. Place on the rim of a glass and pour the cocktail through it or hold it firmly against the rim of the cocktail can or mixing glass and pour from a height.

CITRUS SQUEEZER

Try a hand press (that has the same mechanism as a nutcracker): chop your citrus in half, add to the squeezer and press with all your might. The squeezer will filter out any pips, seeds or stray pith to leave you with a measure of super-fresh juice. Alternatively, you can squeeze a citrus fruit half through your fingers, catching the pips as you go.

CHOPPING BOARD AND KNIFE

Not essential, but it's super useful to have a chopping board and knife specifically for making drinks. Keep the board clean, the knife sharp and practise your citrus-peeling skills: avoid as much pith as possible, leaving just the peel oozing with aromatic oils.

GLASSWARE

BOSTON GLASS

The fancy cousin of the straight-sided pint glass with a slightly flared top. Most Bostons are plain but some are bevelled – such as the IKEA version, which seems to be in every household in the Western world. Great for mixing or using locked into the can of your shaker.

NICK & NORA

Named, inexplicably, after a pair of fictional detectives, this dainty, cute-as-a-button egg-cup-shaped glass on a long stem holds 150–170 ml (5–6 fl oz).

CHAMPAGNE FLUTE

The flute-shaped glass used for Champagne cocktails, Bellinis and Mimosas; hold by pinching at the stem to keep your drink cool and, well, to look as pretentious as possible.

COUPE

The short glass shaped like Marie Antoinette's boob is perfect for Champagne, prosecco and sparkling wines and a more considered alternative to a Martini glass. Vintage versions abound – get a set for your home dive. Holds 150–170 ml (5–6 fl oz), the perfect amount.

FIZZIO

A coupe, Martini glass and a Margarita glass all rolled into one, this pleasingly medium-sized glass has an angular shape and holds a little more than a coupe at 225–265 ml (8–9 fl oz).

MARGARITA

Like a large coupe, the Margarita comes in plain or welled versions with a wide rim for extra rimming (if rimming's your thing).

HIGHBALL

A tall, slightly narrow glass with a pleasingly heavy bottom that holds 225–350 ml (8–12 fl oz) of your favourite long cocktail. A flared version, the Highball Footed (with a short stem and foot), is perhaps a little too fancy for the home dive bar mixer.

MARTINI

Also known as *the* cocktail glass. The long, refined stem and cone-shape vessel flares out to create a wide yet shallow recess. Iconic, impractical (any small gesticulation will have your Espresso Martini sloshing over your sweats) and essential.

HURRICANE

The lamp-shaped classic glass, made for the Hurricane cocktail, is also perfect for long fruity drinks, Tiki concoctions and Bloody Marys. Its impressive size (450–600 ml/15–20 fl oz) helps house all manner of oversized and embarrassing garnishes, from watermelon spears to penis straws.

MOSCOW MULE MUG

The iconic, slightly bulbous copper mug is traditionally used for a Moscow Mule (or should that be a Kyiv Mule?), sometimes a Mojito, or any Tiki-inspired concoction. It forms a delightfully frosty-looking condensation when packed with ice.

OLD FASHIONED

Also known as the Low Ball. From confidently plain to decorative-cut crystal, this short, straight-sided and heavy-bottomed tumbler is perfect for short or single shot drinks. The Rocks is a slight variation: a heavy-bottomed tumbler that flares out slightly. Fancy places have single and double shot versions, plus the Rocks Foot, which has a short stem at the bottom. But really? For the dive bar, any heavy tumbler will do.

TIKI MUG

This curious relic of mid-twentieth-century American Tiki culture (a cocktail movement inspired by booze god Don the Beachcomber), the Tiki Mug is a tall, haunted-looking ceramic mug with a stylised face.

SOUR

Think of the Sour as a small wine glass, fitting about 150–170 ml (5–6 fl oz), bulbous but cute AF. Perfect for Piscos.

COLLINS GLASS

The refined, skinny and usually straight-sided version of the Highball.

SHOT GLASS

Short and simple. Pour, drink, slam down. Done. Also doubles as a temporary jigger.

THE KNACK

SHAKE, FOR ALL OUR SAKES

Ice first, about a third full, then booze and other ingredients. Jam your shaker together and shake. The trick is to be quick and vigorous. There's little consensus in the cocktail world on how long to shake – a few seconds? A whole minute? About seven seconds of dynamic pumping should do it – a frost will spread over the can, your cheeks should wobble, your office lanyard should slap you in the face, and your drink will be ready. Always strain directly into the glass and serve within milliseconds.

1

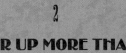

PLEASE BE CHILL

Chill everything: yourself, your glasses, your booze and definitely your mixers. To speed-chill a glass, fill with ice at the start of the drink-making process and discard just before pouring.

3

BE EXACTING

Be more fastidious with your measurements than you think you need to be. A good drink relies on sticking to the rules. Unless you're making a two-ingredient drink, precise quantities are essential.

2

STIR UP MORE THAN STRIFE

Stirring – rather than shaking – minimises dilution, perfect for 100% spirit concoctions. Use your mixing glass, stir drinks gently and confidently with ice to chill the drink. When condensation forms on the outside of the glass and it's feeling frosty, it's ready to serve.

4

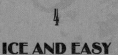

ICE AND EASY

Have more than enough. Then double it. Experiment with classic cubes, oversized mega-cubes, balls and rock ice: freeze still mineral water in a large plastic vessel, tip out onto a clean towel for grip (do not be tempted to steady the block with your other hand) and hack with an ice pick.

THE BACK BAR

The dive bar at home requires a collection of spirits and liqueurs. The perfect back bar houses some mean and lean spirits: a smoky Scotch, a sweet bourbon, a spicy rye, a fragrant gin, a white and spiced rum. You can freeze your vodka and tequila (unless you're sipping them neat), and vermouth, tonic water and beer live in the fridge.

1

BITTERS

Venezuelan (via Trinidad and Tobago) Angostura bitters sit behind ever dive bar in the world. Once thought to be a cure for hiccups, the part-herbal, part-alcoholic tincture has an incredible aroma that gives cocktails a depth of flavour.

2

BOURBON

Bourbon is the whiskey fan's starter spirit, the gateway booze to smoky, slightly creepy spirits down the line. A majority corn mash means more sugar, so think of it as the sweet-natured, youthful American cousin of whiskey.

3

CAMPARI AND APEROL

Sharp, ruby-red Italian bitter aperitifs that pep up cocktails and form the basis of the Negroni and Americano; they are delicious mixed with soda water and chilled sparkling wine.

4
CASSIS

French as anything, crème de cassis or crème de mûre are both dark berry-flavoured liqueurs perfect for Kir Royales – although that's perhaps the last drink you might order at a dive. They're the perfect sweetener in simple gin recipes. Mix a drop of cassis into a G&T to give it a sweet kick and a pink blush.

5
GIN

Gin should be premium enough to sip with tonic. The perfect back bar would have one small batch, handcrafted premium gin and a couple of upscale contenders for mixing.

6
RUM

Traditionally, rum with a dash of lemon or lime was the liquor sailors drank to ward off scurvy. But these days it's less medicinal, more recreational. Brugal Añejo or Zacapa are both upscale, but make sure you have a light rum to hand – it works well in a cocktail.

7
RYE

Like it spicy? In the States, peppery rye whiskey is made from a majority unblended rye mash and aged in charred new oak barrels for at least two years. In Canada, rye is a more general term and might have only a little rye in it, if at all – they really don't mind either way. But what you really need to know is that American rye whiskey is a spicy drop and therefore interesting in cocktails.

8
SCOTCH

Smoky, aged in oak barrels for at least three years, Scottish whisky (in style or provenance), or Scotch, is usually made from malted barley. Single grain means it was made at a single distillery (not necessarily using a single type of grain), and 'single malt' means it's made from a malted grain – again, at a single distillery. Blends – mixes of two or more whiskies, some malted, some not – are deliciously smooth.

9
TEQUILA

Unaged (or aged for no more than 60 days in steel containers) silver (blanco) tequila is an essential part of your back bar. Gold tequila is sweet and smooth enough to sip, and reposado ('rested') tequila, aged in wood-lined tanks or barrels, has a smoky edge.

10
VERMOUTH

A fortified wine, generally Italian, packed with botanicals, in sweet (red), blanc sec (white, the dry side of sweet) and dry (white) versions. Get all three and keep them refrigerated after opening.

11
VODKA

As most dive bars are trapped in the '90s, Absolut (smooth, delicious and just as cool as it was in its formative years) is the most relevant buy here.

12
WHISK(E)Y

Whiskey – with an e – is the Irish and North American version of whisky without an e. It's generally smoother than its feisty Scottish counterpart.

13
TRIPLE SEC AND ORANGE LIQUEUR

Made from the dried peel of sweet and bitter oranges, triple sec is a back bar essential, a bottle of which is the perfect element for many cocktails and will last for aeons.

14
SYRUP

Simple syrup – aka gomme or sugar syrup – is liquid sugar and, when mixed part-for-part with sharp citrus juices, brings a sweet-sour note to a recipe. It's a back bar essential.

STONEWALL INN

New York,
USA

To Greenwich Village, NYC, and a little dive bar that has punched firmly above its weight since 1930. The Stonewall Inn has survived prohibition, a location change and police raids from its time as a speakeasy to the night-time refuge of disenfranchised queer New Yorkers, and still it pours on. By the mid '60s Stonewall had earned itself a set of dubious Mafia investors who turned it into a gay bar. The owners despised their queer patrons who were blackmailed or – even worse – served watered-down drinks, and yet queer New Yorkers had few other places to go; they were generally safer inside Stonewall than out.

In 1969, after months of tension between the clientele, the owners and the police, things were at fever pitch. One night, and after one police raid too many, the LGBTQ+ crowd pushed back. What followed was a haphazard, riotous and at-times violent three-day standoff between the local queer community and the police. Stonewall wasn't the beginning of queer resistance in the US (the first major queer pushback seems to have been at Cooper Do-Nuts in Los Angeles in 1959), and nor was it the last, but it's the most well-known and it inspired a mass movement of LGBTQ+ liberation. On 28 June 1999, in honour of the 30th anniversary of the riots, the Stonewall Inn was added to the US National Register of Historic Places.

Today, Stonewall has settled into its new status as a beloved national monument the only way it knows how: drag nights, bingo, piano singalongs, drinks promotions and merch. It's the epicentre of the Village's LGBTQ+ scene and often the first stop for any fresh-faced gay, lesbian, bi or trans traveller new to the city in search of queer history, community, a Grindr hookup or just a cold beer ('til 4am, seven days a week).

01

FERRARI

Glass	Serves	Vibe
Old Fashioned	1	Stern Italian Nonna Lets Her Hair Down

INGREDIENTS

45 ml (1½ fl oz) Fernet-Branca
45 ml (1½ fl oz) Campari
Orange twist (optional)
Large ice cube
Orange twist (optional)

EQUIPMENT

Jigger
Mixing glass
Bar spoon
Cocktail strainer

Also known as the 'bartender's handshake' the Ferrari is a delicious and dirty-tasting double amaro cocktail that will put hair on your chest. A powerful little sipper of Fernet-Branca and Campari, this is a simple two-shotter (the name Ferrari is a portmanteau of its ingredients, of course). You'll know Campari, the acid-red bitter aperitivo with sweet citrus tones, but Fernet is its impossibly medicinal, menthol and bittermint cousin you learn to love. Fernet-Branca, concocted by Italian herbalist Bernardino Branca, met its first pair of unsuspecting lips in the mid 1800s. It's been thought of as a cure-all ever since . . . or a kill-all, depending on who you're drinking with. Once a worm-killer and period-pain soother, F-B was a must-have in prohibition-era New York City, sold in pharmacies as a medicine. But mixed with Campari (or served long, with cola) is Fernet-Branca's spiritual home.

1   Chill an old fashioned glass for at least 20 minutes.

2   Fill a mixing glass two-thirds full with ice.

3   Add the Fernet and Campari.

4   Stir briskly (or lazily, no one will know) for 20 seconds or so.

5   Strain into the glass over ice – preferably one large, unwieldly cube – and serve. Orange twist optional.

AMERICANO

Glass	Serves	Theme Tune
Old Fashioned	1	'Tu Vuò' fà L'Americano' by Renato Carosone

INGREDIENTS

45 ml (1½ fl oz) Campari

45 ml (1½ fl oz) sweet vermouth

Classic ice cubes

Lemon slice

30–60 ml (1–2 fl oz) soda water, chilled, to top

EQUIPMENT

Jigger

Pre- and post-war Italy was in thrall to American culture, and 'Tu Vuò' fà L'Americano' – and the Americano cocktail itself – are both nods towards Italo-American love. 'Tu Vuò' fà L'Americano', aka 'You Want to Play American', is the peppy 1950s Italian pop song that underpins the sizzling nightclub set piece in gorgeous late '90s thriller *The Talented Mr. Ripley*. Matt Damon (the film's duplicitous but handsome antagonist) sings the song with Italian personality Rosario Fiorello and Jude Law (playing a spoiled, rich American) – and the crowd goes wild (incidentally, the costume notes for Jude Law were to go commando in every scene and you can absolutely tell).

The first version of the Campari and sweet vermouth concoction was served at Gaspare Campari's bar in Milan in the 1860s but under a different name: the Milano-Torino. It was renamed the Americano decades later, inspired by expat Americans' love of the delicious recipe. It's a thirst-quencher, best served with extra-chilled club soda on the side, creating an almost never-ending drink.

1   Add Campari and sweet vermouth to an old fashioned glass over ice.

2   Tuck in the lemon slice, top with chilled soda water, and serve.

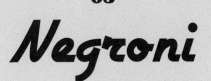

Negroni

Glass	Serves	Theme Tune
Old Fashioned	1	'That's Amore' by Dean Martin

INGREDIENTS

30 ml (1 fl oz) Campari

30 ml (1 fl oz) sweet vermouth

30 ml (1 fl oz) gin

Classic ice cubes & large cube

Orange slice

EQUIPMENT

Jigger

Mixing glass

Bar spoon

Cocktail strainer

A few years ago there were those who claimed the Negroni was too high brow to be associated with the classic dive bar, but much has changed. Dive drinkers are now happy to chug back glass after ruby-hued glass without embarrassment as they flick through laminated karaoke folders, secretly vape weed under their Balenciaga hoodies and flick salted peanuts at friends who have dozed off. The drink has entered the dive bar consciousness and we are all the better for it.

Like all cocktail origin stories, the legend of the Negroni is murky, but it is thought to be a simplified version of the Americano, requested by a certain gadfly Count Camillo Negroni at Cafe Casoni in Florence around 1919. The obliging bartender, Forsco Scarselli, had a genius idea and swapped out the Americano's chilled soda water for gin – and Count Negroni's Negroni was born. Its confident simplicity – equal parts gin, sweet vermouth and Campari – means that when the moon hits your eye like a big pizza pie, this is the perfect drink to mix at home. A stir in a mixing glass is best but building the Negroni in its serving glass is also acceptable. The classic version calls for a fat wedge of orange, but an orange twist will do.

1   Add Campari, sweet vermouth and gin to a mixing glass with ice.

2   Stir an strain into an old fashioned glass with a large ice cube.

3   Add an orange slice and serve. Alternatively, build in the serving glass, add a large ice cube, and serve.

NEGRONI BIANCO

Glass	*Serves*	*Vibe*
Old Fashioned	1	Kind of Embarrassed You Love *Emily in Paris*

INGREDIENTS

20 ml (¾ fl oz) Lillet Blanc

30 ml (1 fl oz) gin

20 ml (¾ fl oz) Suze or Luxardo

Classic ice cubes, plus 1 large cube

Grapefruit slice (white or pink)

EQUIPMENT

Jigger

Mixing glass

Bar spoon

Cocktail strainer

BARTENDER'S NOTE

For a quicker mix you can build in the serving glass, add a large ice cube, and serve.

The Negroni Bianco, aka the White Negroni, is a deliciously modern concoction attributed to British bartender Wayne Collins. In 2001 he found himself on a steamy summer trip in Bordeaux, where – in looking for the ingredients of the classic Campari Negroni – the local bottle shop offered up alternative inspiration. He used purely French spirits to create an homage to the original, and the result expanded the NCU (Negroni Classic Universe) forever. If you like Campari then you'll like its rather memorable French cousin Suze, the pale golden-yellow French aperitif that's just as bitter-sweet and citrusy as its clown's-nose-coloured counterpart. It's subtler too, so whichever gin you use will stand out (so invest in a good one). Lillet Blanc is the French vermouth-like fortified wine that's floral and herbal and quite out there for the usual Negroni drinker. Both Suze and Lillet Blanc are stalwarts of the Francophile dive bar scene.

Since Collins created the Negroni Bianco, the drink has been reworked and reimagined a number of times, but purists like to stay true to Collins' favourite citrus garnish, the grapefruit, and the home dive-bar mixer would be wise to do the same.

1   Add Lillet Blanc, Suze and gin to a mixing glass with ice.

2   Stir and strain into an old fashioned glass with a large ice cube.

3   Add a grapefruit slice (white or pink) and serve.

05

LONG ISLAND ICED TEA

Glass	Serves	Theme Tune
Highball and Pitcher	4	'O.G. Original Gangster' by Ice-T

INGREDIENTS

60 ml (2 fl oz) gin

60 ml (2 fl oz) vodka

60 ml (2 fl oz) rum

60 ml (2 fl oz) tequila

60 ml (2 fl oz) triple sec

60 ml (2 fl oz) fresh lemon juice

60 ml (2 fl oz) simple syrup

180 ml (6 fl oz) cola

4–6 fresh lemon slices

Classic ice cubes

EQUIPMENT

Jigger

Pitcher

Bar spoon

BARTENDER'S NOTE

Try your own late-night tweaks with white or dark rum, tequila or mezcal, but don't leave out the triple sec – the orange liquor is the only element elevating the LIIT from bucket of booze to delightfully drinkable.

There's a war going on in cocktail land, a clash of the titans in a glass: Tennessee and New York both lay claim to being the birthplace of the insanely boozy Long Island Iced Tea. The city of Kingsport, TN, say the dive-bar favourite was indeed created on Long Island, but Long Island, Tennessee, a tiny island on the Holston River, near Kingsport. There, it is claimed, a local moonshiner, Charlie 'Old Man' Bishop, created one of his infamous 'special batches' in the 1920s, mixing vodka, rum, whiskey, tequila and gin . . . with a little maple syrup for good measure. By the 1940s he had apparently updated the recipe, adding lime and cola or soda, making it startlingly like the LIIT we know and love today, minus the triple sec.

New York, of course, is having none of it. NYers point out Robert 'Rosebud' Butt's recipe was created as part of a cocktail contest on Long Island, NY, in the 1970s. Whoever is right, the Long Island Iced Tea remains a dive-bar stalwart and, thankfully, requires very little finesse to create at home. The deceptive and delicious long drink is sweet (and dangerously strong – but don't let that stop you) and a total crowd pleaser. This is the pitcher recipe, serving four lucky Long Islanders.

1   Add the liquids – apart from the cola – and lemon slices to a pitcher filled two-thirds full with ice and stir.

2   Top with the cola and stir again, slowly, and serve.

CHEZ JEANNETTE

Paris,
France

Let's head to rue du Faubourg Saint-Denis in Paris, France, home to fancy wig shops, delicious Turkish eateries and the city's first Arc de Triomphe, built in the 17th century. There, on a corner – littered with chairs and tables and slouching young things in clouds of vape, Byredo fragrances and *Gauloises* smoke – is Chez Jeannette, the city's most beloved dive bar. Although a working bar for decades, Chez Jeannette drew wider attention in 2007 when the Jeannette in question sold the site to a new, young crew who promised to preserve its unique character. They haven't changed a thing (or so the legend goes): the interior is wonderfully worn and inviting, with a chrome bar and sallow, ornate ceilings, sconce lamps, a dusty chandelier, tarnished mirror tiles, red pleather banquettes and that icon of Paris: the dubious bathroom.

It's a particularly refreshing spot in a city with an excess of glittering drinking palaces and idiosyncratic cocktail bars, all set-dressed purely *pour le Instagram*. There's a simple menu, a small and classic cocktail list and prices are good, but it's the indefinable atmosphere that's Chez Jeannette's real USP – and *merde*, is it ever popular! You'll be lucky to get a seat in the end-of-the-week after-work rush, but on other nights your own little corner of Jeannette's is comfortably won. You'll start with a Moscow Mule, perhaps, and then wine and *steak-frites*, and a candle will be placed on your battered Formica bistro table when the house lights are dimmed. *C'est paradis*!

Paris a little too far for the perfect dive? Statesiders have their own version in Le Dive, a delightful drinking spot in NYC – a Dimes Square ode to Chez Jeannette on the Lower East Side.

COSMOPOLITAN

Glass	Serves	Vibe
Martini, Coupe or Nick & Nora	1	Wistful Nostalgic Sadness at a *SATC*-Themed Mature-Bride-To-Be Bachelorette Party

INGREDIENTS

45 ml (1½ fl oz) citrus vodka (lemon is best)

20 ml (¾ fl oz) Cointreau

20 ml (¾ fl oz) fresh lime juice (yes, it seems a bit much, but go with it)

15 ml (½ fl oz) cranberry juice (just a hint, really)

Classic ice cubes

Lime twist

EQUIPMENT

Jigger

BARTENDER'S NOTE

Cranberry juice adds the famous Cosmo colour, but you don't have to make it as bright as possible; feel free to turn it down to a more simple, classy tone . . . which is *such* a Miranda thing to say.

This iconic 1990s Martini-like cocktail is unerringly pretty (pale peony pink to ruby-toned, depending on how you make it) and is synonymous with New York City nightlife, illicit midnight kisses, broken hearts and heels. The Cosmopolitan's guest-star appearance in legendary HBO show *Sex and the City* made it the go-to drink for every Carrie Bradshaw wannabe around the globe, a direct line to a fantastically moneyed and messy Manhattan lifestyle most of us could otherwise only dream about. By the 2000s the Cosmo had somewhat peaked and soon fell out of favour, finding a new home: at the dive bar. And there it has lived, happily and rather sexily, ever since.

As cocktail land's most misunderstood drink, the Cosmo is surprisingly grown up: it's drier and sourer than sweet and sickly, and it's perfectly balanced. In the mid '80s vodka became king of the cocktail world; Absolut Citron was the must-have spirit, and the race was on to create the perfect recipe to let it sing. There are many claims to the Cosmopolitan's provenance. Was it invented by Dale DeGroff in 1988 at New York City's Rainbow Room, or Toby Cecchini across town at the Odeon? Or was it first poured by legendary bartender Cheryl Cook at Miami's The Strand in 1985? Whoever it was, the combination of citrus vodka, cranberry, lots of fresh lime juice and a touch of orange-scented Cointreau is a delightful and enduring idea.

1   Combine vodka, Cointreau, fresh lime juice and cranberry juice in a cocktail shaker over ice, and shake vigorously until frosty.

2   Strain into a martini glass, coupe or a Nick & Nora. Add a lime twist and serve.

THE PERFECT GIN & TONIC

Glass	Serves	Snack
Highball or Old Fashioned	1	Ridged Potato Chips and Hot Sauce or Acid-Bright Cheetos Variant

INGREDIENTS

45 ml (1½ fl oz) gin (over-pour, just a little)

Classic ice cubes

Pink grapefruit slice

Tonic water, to top (chilled, and not 'light')

EQUIPMENT

Jigger

In the late 1600s London was awash with wastrels. William of Orange had relaxed the capital's alcohol licensing laws, meaning booze could be distilled near-anywhere. Dive bars soon sprung up, and the city was grappling with a binge-drinking crisis from which it has never truly recovered. At the centre of the scandal was gin, the 'quick flash of lightning', but it wasn't until the 1800s that it met its forever friend: tonic water. Quinine, a bitter-tasting anti-malarial, was being mixed with sugar and gin in the hot places those problematic, colonial Brits found themselves, and on returning to London, the demand for a similar recipe grew. Gin and mixers soon evolved into classy long drinks and clever cocktails, and the Gin and Tonic was born.

The humble Gin and Tonic is now a mainstay of every dive in the world, a foolhardy and fresh hit of sweet bitterness in a long, chilled glass. Of course, with something so simple, it's easy to get it wrong. An unfortunate gin, perhaps, or a weak and barely bubbly tonic water can ruin one of life's pleasures. But get it right and it's delicious. Oh, and a word about your mixer. There are all manner of gourmet tonic waters in the world, but this book is going out on a limb to say that the old-school original, the O.G. and G.O.A.T., is still the best: Schweppes. Its sweet bitterness is perfectly balanced and its fizz (dispensed from a small can or mini glass bottle, and never a crusty soda gun) is intense and lively. And it's unpretentious. Isn't that just what we want when we're chugging back a G&T while we're waiting for the pool table to come free?

1   Add gin to a glass filled two-thirds with ice.

2   Tuck in a pink grapefruit slice (cut it as annoyingly big and juicy as possible), top with chilled tonic water, and serve.

BOILERMAKER

Glass	Serves	Theme Tune
American Pint & Shot	1	'9 to 5' by Dolly Parton

INGREDIENTS

45 ml (1½ fl oz) whiskey

1 American pint of lager, extra cold

The ultimate dive bar cocktail, although the word 'cocktail' might be building up the Boilermaker somewhat. But it's the drink that has been poured, sipped and slammed down on sticky bar tops since the 1800s, or so the legend goes. This wonderfully straight-forward pairing of whiskey (neat, in a shot glass) and a cold beer can be either mixed (the ritual goes: big beer-gulp, pour in whiskey, slowly sup-up) or enjoyed swiftly and separately by downing the whiskey and enjoying the beer as a refreshing chaser. It is thought the Boilermaker was the drink order *du jour* for US factory workers in the 1800s who, at the end of their shift, would request a shot and a beer to cure their workday woes. The Boilermaker has been a part of dive-bar culture to this day. In fact, when contemporary bartenders and cocktail tastemakers are asked what they might order in their local dive, they almost always pick the Boilermaker, perhaps out of fear rather than desire. There's safety in a simple shot and pint of draught beer.

Bourbon or rye works well with a pale, light beer, or a smoky, peaty whiskey pairs best with an IPA. If you're (responsibly) enjoying your BM in two parts, good luck to you. If, indeed, you would like to perform some bar-top alchemy, drink down your beer by around a third and drop in your full shot glass of whiskey; you'll have made some booze magic. An alternative is the fascinating Dr Pepper Bomb: a shot of amaretto and half a pint of beer poured into a pint glass with a splash of cola. Drop in your amaretto shot glass and you'll have made an oddly delicious drink (that only makes sense at 2am).

1   Pour both drinks.

2   Gulp down your shot and sip your beer, or fill your American pint glass two-thirds full and let the drinker drop in – or pour – their own shot of whiskey. Sit back and be part of dive bar history.

MOSCOW MULE

Glass	*Serves*	*Reading Matter*
Copper Mug	1	*Animal Farm* by George Orwell

INGREDIENTS

Crushed ice cubes

45 ml (1½ fl oz) vodka, chilled

15 ml (½ fl oz) freshly squeezed lime juice

135 ml (4½ fl oz) ginger beer, chilled

Lime wedge

EQUIPMENT

Jigger

BARTENDER'S NOTE

Ginger beer is spicier and stronger than ginger ale – and the Mule is all the better for it.

The Moscow Mule came abruptly into being in New York in 1941, mixed by John 'Jack' Morgan at the Chatham Hotel on Vanderbilt Avenue, near East 48th Street – a long-since demolished beacon of Gilded Age architecture. Morgan and his Smirnoff rep friend John Martin were lamenting the slow rise in vodka interest and set about experimenting with new, easy recipes to get New Yorkers lit on the clear stuff. Now, the Chatham was hardly a dive, but Morgan's cocktail – vodka, ginger beer and lime juice – and its slutty simplicity soon made it a stalwart of the dive-bar scene. They hastily named it the Moscow Mule (after vodka's Russian roots and in reference to the fiery mule's kick of ginger beer) and set about making it the talk of the town.

Martin is even credited with the Mule's trademark copper mug – he'd lug a set of them around in the years after the Mule was born, showing them off to bartenders – and the mug eventually became synonymous with Martin and Morgan's recipe.

One thing: being a purely American rather than Russian invention, the Mule might be easily renamed without any fear of cultural insensitivity. A different city might be swapped in, Kyiv, perhaps?

1   Add ice to a copper mug, about half to two-thirds full.

2   Add vodka and lime juice, then top with ginger beer.

3   Add a lime wedge to garnish.

10

MANHATTAN

Glass	Serves	Essential Viewing
Nick & Nora or Coupe	1	Seinfeld, Seasons 1 to 9

INGREDIENTS

Classic ice cubes
60 ml (2 fl oz) rye whiskey
30 ml (1 fl oz) sweet vermouth
2 dashes Angostura bitters
1 dash orange bitters
Brandied cherry or lemon twist

EQUIPMENT

Jigger
Mixing glass
Bar spoon
Cocktail strainer
Cocktail stick (optional)

BARTENDER'S NOTE

The brandied cherry elevates the drink and gives those for whom rye is a little too intense a sweet treat.

This rye-fuelled classic was, at one point, the world's most famous and beloved cocktail; the Negroni of its day, if you will. In fact, like the Negroni, the Manhattan's essential ingredient is Italian vermouth, but it's the spicy American rye whiskey that gives the recipe its sturdy, slap-you-in-the-face NYC taste. It looks gorgeous, too: all cherries and rust.

Although its exact provenance is unclear, there are mentions of the Manhattan dating from the late 1800s, and it has barely changed over its more than 140 years of being swigged everywhere from the most glittering cocktail palaces to the diveiest dives. That said, there are variations: the so-called Perfect Manhattan is a subtle tweak on the original, somewhat drier and delicately pale, mixing dry and sweet vermouth (instead of a full ounce of sweet vermouth), and others recommend a dash of orange bitters (as here) or even replacing Angostura with orange bitters entirely.

1 Fill a mixing glass two-thirds with ice.

2 Add the rye, vermouth and bitters and stir for 30 seconds.

3 Strain into a chilled Nick & Nora glass or coupe, add your lemon twist (classy) or balance a brandied cherry on a cocktail stick across the rim of the glass (classiest).

11

Bloody Mary

Glass	Serves	Karaoke Track
Highball	1	'Spice Up Your Life' by The Spice Girls

INGREDIENTS

Classic ice cubes

60 ml (2 fl oz) vodka, chilled

15 ml (½ fl oz) freshly squeezed lemon juice

150 ml (5 fl oz) tomato juice, chilled

3 drops Worcestershire sauce

2–3 drops Tabasco

Pinch celery salt

Pinch black pepper

Pinch cayenne pepper

Lemon wedge to garnish

Two garlicky green olives, pitted, sharing a cocktail stick

Large and leafy celery stick

EQUIPMENT

Jigger

Classic ice cubes

Bar spoon

Paper or re-usable straw

Who is the guilty party responsible for the Bloody Mary, the oddly moreish savoury concoction beloved of the hungover? Was it Fernand Petiot, one-time barman of Harry's New York Bar in 1920s Paris, or did he merely add a little heat to an existing recipe? Harry's was, at the time, one of the coolest bars in the world, attracting an impressive celeb clientele, from Rita Hayworth to Humphry Bogart, and Petiot was its master of the dark arts. Apparently he took the humble two-element cocktail of vodka and tomato juice and added a little spice, citrus juice and – later in his career – Tabasco. Like a rock star Petiot moved to new venues, taking his concoctions with him, until he settled in New York City, spreading the popularity of drinks like the Bloody Mary. But many booze historians are confident the true inventor is George Jessel, Hollywood actor and lover of all things booze, who wrote an earlier anecdote about how he and a bartender friend devised the recipe during a night of across-the-bar shenanigans.

For such an apparently complicated recipe, most dive bars are happy to make a Bloody Mary of sorts, and the drink's endless tweaks and permutations have made it one of the most idiosyncratic orders known to drinkers – everyone has their favourite version. Add-ons include freshly grated horseradish, cornichons, pickle juice, Dijon mustard, a splash of white wine, your hopes and dreams . . . anything.

1   Fill a highball with ice two-thirds to three-quarters full.

2   Add vodka and lemon juice, and top with tomato juice.

3   Add the Worcestershire sauce, Tabasco, celery salt and black pepper. Stir well.

4   Finish with the cayenne pepper, lemon wedge, olives and celery stick. Serve with a straw.

B.Y.G.

Tokyo,
Japan

Let's head to 1969, Shibuya, Tokyo. The smooth yacht rock sounds of local pop group Happy End are drifting out from their unofficial home: notoriously cute dive bar B.Y.G. (Beautiful Young Generation). On a narrow pedestrianised alleyway, minutes from the Hachiko memorial statue at Shibuya station and in among the 'love hotels', this welcoming bar was originally a live music venue, and today it houses three shadowy floors panelled in wood, music posters, stickers, piles of CDs, records and paper slips (to write down your classic rock requests for the in-house DJ).

These days, B.Y.G. is more of a music café, but little has really changed in the last few decades, and the sounds of Led Zep, Dylan, and The Velvet Underground are still on rotation. When rock music first came to Japan in the mid '60s, B.Y.G. was its spiritual home, and super-group Happy End formed the same year the venue opened. At that time, bars and cafés with the type of PA system that could house rock bands with electric guitars were few and far between. B.Y.G. changed all that and helped underpin Japan's obsession with US-influenced rock.

The venue's founders took its name from a European jazz record label; 'Beautiful Young Generation' just seemed to fit. Today, the crowd is delightfully mixed, with old timers keen to relive their youth and the youths who love the dive's gnarly authenticity.

12

BLOODY MARIA and HER SISTERS

Glass	*Serves*	*Karaoke Track*
Highball	1	'Sisters Are Doing It for Themselves' by Eurythmics and Aretha Franklin

INGREDIENTS

Lemon wedge

Salt and cayenne pepper
  to rim the glass

Classic ice cubes

60 ml (2 fl oz) tequila, chilled

15 ml (½ fl oz) freshly squeezed
  lemon juice

150 ml (5 fl oz) tomato
  juice, chilled

3 drops Worcestershire sauce

2–3 drops Tabasco

Pinch celery salt

Pinch black pepper

Two jalapeño slices
  on a cocktail stick

Large and leafy celery stick

EQUIPMENT

Jigger

Bar spoon

Paper or re-usable straw

Swap out the vodka in a classic Bloody Mary for another spirit and you have the beginnings of something else entirely. The Bloody Maria uses tequila as its booze power punch, but she has a coterie of complicated sisters who also like their time in the spotlight. The Red Snapper is gin based, giving a botanical finish to the drink, and the Bloody Caesar is made with clamato juice, a blend of tomato juice and dried clam broth, which – to those unfamiliar – sounds hellish but is umami-rich and delicious. The Green Mary uses tomatillo juice for a slime-toned hue, the Bloody Marianne uses bourbon as its star ingredient, and the Bloody Bull – somewhat improbably – uses bone broth as its USP.

1   Run the lemon wedge around the rim of a highball and dip into a mixture of salt and cayenne pepper.

2   Fill with ice half to two-thirds full. Add tequila and lemon juice and top with tomato juice.

3   Add the Worcestershire sauce, Tabasco, celery salt and black pepper. Stir well.

4   Finish with the lemon wedge, jalapeño and celery stick. Serve with a straw.

13

DAIQUIRI

Glass	*Serves*	*Essential Reading*
Coupe	1	*For Whom the Bell Tolls* by Ernest Hemingway

INGREDIENTS

Classic ice cubes
60 ml (2 fl oz) white rum
20 ml (¾ fl oz) fresh lime juice
15–20 ml (½–¾ fl oz)
    simple syrup
Lime twist or wheel

EQUIPMENT

Jigger
Shaker
Cocktail strainer

The Daiquiri is the iconic sour rum, citrus and sugar three-way that's been the downfall of many, not least Ernest Hemingway, the six-toed cat lover and Nobel-winning American author of *For Whom the Bell Tolls*. The great Hemingway loved Daiquiris so much he ended up with a boozy spin-off named after him. For the original, you'll need white rum, a freshly squeezed lime (or two) and some simple syrup, but for a Hemingway, you'll need to add maraschino cherry liqueur and a little grapefruit juice, adding a warm blush. It's heady, to the point and – much like a Martini or Margarita – will get you down and dirty within the hour.

There is another side to the Daiquiri: a sassy, fruity, LED-flashing ice cube aspect many hardened cocktail snobs look down on. Some love to blend their 'D' with ice and add fresh strawberries or pineapple, creating a drink the consistency of fro-yo, then adding a floral garnish or penis-straw. It's easy to roll one's eyes at such a drink, but woah are they delicious! Either way, the Daiquiri works best when it's extra chilled and the citrus is as fresh as can be.

1   Fill your coupe with ice to chill it.

2   Add the rum, lime juice and simple syrup – and the ice from the coupe – to a cocktail shaker. Shake for the time it takes to say 'six-toed-cat' five times.

3   Strain and pour. Add a lime twist or wheel and serve.

14

CUBA LIBRE

Glass	Serves	Essential Reading
Collins	1	*Before Night Falls* by Reinaldo Arenas

INGREDIENTS

Classic ice cubes

15 ml (½ fl oz) lime juice, freshly squeezed

2 drops Angostura bitters

60 ml (2 fl oz) light rum, a really good one

Coca-cola, full calorie and chilled, to top

Lime wedge

EQUIPMENT

Jigger

The eagle-eyed among you will note that the Cuba Libre is merely a hastily put together rum and coke – the student staple – but its history is rich with revolution. 'Cuba libre!' was the battle cry heard on the streets of Havana during the Ten Years' War (1868–1878), when Cuba sought freedom from Spanish occupation. Soldiers would shout 'Free Cuba!' and sip a dark rum with molasses or honey. Eventually Spain conceded, and American businesses hopped excitedly across the water to peddle their wares. Coca-Cola syrup arrived in Cuba in 1902 and was a sure-fire hit. Soon after, the syrup made its way into what had become the national drink, the Cuba Libre. The rum itself was distilled by Bacardi, Cuba's iconic booze brand based in Santiago di Cuba that feels almost essential for the modern version of the Cuba Libre that uses Coca-Cola soda rather than syrup (which, incidentally, is not available in Cuba – or North Korea, for that matter). Today the Cuba Libre remains the go-to for feverishly excitable college kids who want to get lit with real Cuban freedom, but don't feel too pretentious to upgrade via a very fine rum, extra lime or a gourmet cola; just remember to shout your revolutionary battle cry before you take your first sip.

1   Fill your Collins two-thirds full with ice.

2   Add the lime juice, Angostura and rum and top – slowly – with cola.

3   Add a lime wedge to garnish; run the lime around the rim of glass if you're that way inclined.

15

Greyhound

Glass	*Serves*	*Karaoke Track*
Old Fashioned	1	'I Wanna Be Your Dog' by The Stooges

INGREDIENTS

Large ice cubes

45 ml (1½ fl oz) vodka or gin, chilled

Freshly squeezed grapefruit juice, chilled, to top

Lime wedge

EQUIPMENT

Jigger

Does your local dive allow dogs? Is it officially mutt-friendly, with dog biscuits in a jar and canine hair on the velvet banquette? Or is it at least 'dog-blind' (so you can you sneak in an aged Chihuahua or bichon frisé under your jacket and the bartender will ignore your transgression)? If so, it's a dive worth diving into. Why? Because dogs are near magic. And they shouldn't be deprived of the delights of dive bar culture. Celebrate humankind's most faithful poop-machine with the Greyhound, the classic cocktail as simple-minded and speedy as its namesake.

The heavenly combination of gin or vodka and grapefruit juice with ice is the perfect slap-in-the-face drink; a sort of evil Mimosa, if you will. It first appeared in Harry Craddock's *Savoy Cocktail Book* from 1930, but Smirnoff's success in New York in the 1950s saw the Greyhound take on vodka as its base, and the old dog is now made primarily with the Russian stuff. A word of warning: boxed or bottled juice is notably not as delicious as freshly squeezed. Try pink grapefruit for a slightly sweeter drink or salt the rim to make a Salty Dog. And if your own beloved canine cocks its leg and leaves its own little concoction on the karaoke machine, just make like a greyhound and get out of there – fast.

1   Fill your glass with a couple of large ice cubes.

2   Add vodka or gin and top with grapefruit juice.

3   Add a lime wedge to garnish. Lap it up like a dog.

16

MARGARITA

Glass	Serves	Essential Reading
Margarita or Old Fashioned	1	*The Master and Margarita* by Mikhail Bulgakov

INGREDIENTS

Lime wedge and lime wheel

Flaked salt for rimming

60 ml (2 fl oz) tequila blanco

30 ml (1 fl oz) freshly squeezed lime juice

15 ml (½ fl oz) orange liqueur (triple sec, Cointreau, Grand Marnier)

15 ml (½ fl oz) agave syrup

Classic ice cubes

EQUIPMENT

Saucer

Jigger

Shaker

Cocktail strainer

There are, of course, myriad and magical ways to enjoy tequila, Mexico's premier spirit. Sipped delicately over cracked ice; frozen and sucked through a penis straw at your nephew's gender-reveal party; downed in one wet, leering gulp from a plastic shot glass at 3am; or in the perfect Margarita, one of the world's most popular and fresh-tasting cocktails. The sour sharpness of freshly squeezed lime juice, the sweetness of orange liqueur and the power-punch of tequila are the Margarita's bones, but most home-mixers like to add their own little something to make it their own. Some swap out the orange liqueur for simple or agave syrup (which, although a little basic, can be just as delicious as the original); others use Mezcal – tequila's naughty cousin – with its smoky, earthy tone. But it's the original that the dive-drinker must learn to master. There are a few ground rules: the tequila blanco must be 100% blue agave; the lime must be freshly squeezed; the desire to lose 1½ hours of your life must be authentic and whole-hearted.

1. Run the lime wedge around the edge of the glass and dip into a saucer of salt.

2. Add the tequila, lime juice, orange liqueur and agave syrup to a shaker, filled with ice.

3. Shake until frosty and strain into the glass.

4. Add the lime wheel to garnish.

SALTY DAWG SALOON

Alaska, USA

The saloon at the end of the world, the Salty Dog is a tiny log cabin of a place, but its fame in Homer, Alaska, nay the world, is outsized. Built in 1897, and one of the first buildings in the township of Homer, the Salty Dawg has served its community in many guises, from post office to railroad station to family home. By 1957 the Dawg was ready for its next iteration, as a saloon, and was moved in 1964 to its present location on Homer Spit – with water either side of it – after an earthquake. Around the same time, an unsightly water tower next to the Dawg was disguised as a lighthouse – and together they became Homer's most memorable landmark.

Visit today and you'll be charmed by the Salty Dawg and Homer Spit itself – decorated with hand-painted signs, wind chimes, trinkets and the latest fishy haul (it's a working port); it's as if the dive bar interior has seeped out of the Dawg itself. Inside you'll see (thousands?) of dollar bills pinned to its walls, each signed by a drinker wanting to leave a little something of themselves at this remote outpost of dive culture. Knowing the Dawg's history underlines how important the bar is to the community of Homer and how resilient it is – something the locals share with the Dawg itself.

17

FRENCH 75

Glass	Serves	Essential Watching
Champagne Flute or Coupe	1	*Emily in Paris*, all seasons, not an episode skipped

INGREDIENTS

60 ml (2 fl oz) gin or cognac

15 ml (½ fl oz) freshly squeezed lemon juice

15 ml (½ fl oz) simple syrup

Classic ice cubes

Champagne, chilled, to top

EQUIPMENT

Jigger

Shaker

Cocktail strainer

The history of the French 75 is deliciously tense. Booze historians and cocktail bores will argue for hours over its birth date and place, and who its true inventor might be. It's best to leave them arguing at the bar and claim a spot between the mounted animatronic bass and Coolidge's 'Dogs Playing Poker' and set about working up a chic, Parisian vibe. This gin, lemon, sugar and Champagne cocktail – served audaciously in a champagne flute – is a tour de force. Let's settle on the Soixante-Quinze being a post-WWI drink that grew in popularity in the 1920s, probably at Harry's New York Bar in Paris, where it was claimed the drink gave a kick like a French 75mm field gun. And the French 75 itself is quite something – it's tart, boozy and long like a Mimosa, only with far bigger *couilles*.

1   Chill a champagne flute or coupe.

2   Shake the gin or cognac, lemon juice and simple syrup over ice.

3   Strain into the glass and top with Champagne.

18

GIMLET

Glass	Serves	Karaoke Track
Coupe	1	'Gin and Juice' by Snoop Dogg

INGREDIENTS

75 ml (2½ fl oz) gin

15 ml (½ fl oz) freshly squeezed lime juice

15 ml (½ fl oz) simple syrup

Classic ice cubes

Lime wheel

EQUIPMENT

Jigger

Shaker

Cocktail strainer

The Gimlet might not have been the drink Snoop Dogg was dreaming about when penning his 1994 mega-hit 'Gin and Juice', but it sure fits the bill. An erstwhile poet, Snoop's retelling of a bawdy teenage party – powered by weed, desire and the aforementioned gin and juice – is the perfect set-up to enjoy this moreish and strong-edged drink.

The Gimlet is a gin sour, like the Daiquiri in both method, ingredients and simplicity. Gin is the spirit in question, and the juice is traditionally freshly squeezed lime. There are nods to 18th-century naval history in both the Gimlet and Daiquiri's origin stories: the idea being that sailors loved nothing more than booze and warding off scurvy. But doesn't this typecast our beloved ancient seamen? Isn't it sailorphobic, in fact?

Best to think of Harry Craddock's booze bible, *The Savoy Cocktail Book* (1930) as the Gimlet's first appearance at the bar (with Snoop's 1994 song a turning point). For years, the lime had a sweet stand-in with Rose's Lime Cordial, but contemporary Gimlets insist on the fresh stuff, with a little simple syrup to take the edge off. Shake, pour and get laid back, with your mind on your money and your money on your mind.

1   Shake the gin (Snoop suggests Tanqueray), juice (lime) and simple syrup over ice until frosty.

2   Strain into a chilled coupe.

3   Add lime wheel to garnish.

19

Tom Collins

Glass	Serves	Karaoke Track
Collins	1	'Who's That Girl' by Madonna

INGREDIENTS

Classic ice cubes

60 ml (2 fl oz) gin

15 ml (½ fl oz) freshly squeezed lemon juice

15 ml (½ fl oz) simple syrup

Chilled soda water, to top

Lemon wheel

EQUIPMENT

Jigger

Shaker

Cocktail strainer

Named after a mysterious, internationally renowned asshat; a man who would haunt the cocktail bars and dives of New York, Philadelphia, London and Paris and slander their patrons before heading off to do it all again somewhere else. His poisoned barbs would be delivered to each bartender, who would have the unenviable job of passing on his salty tales when the drinker next took up his or her regular spot at the bar: 'You know a guy called Tom Collins? He was *just* in here bad-mouthing you' . . . or so the legend goes. Things reached fever pitch in 1874 with the story hitting the papers and drinkers baying for poor Collins' blood.

Of course, there never was a Tom Collins. Or at least, not of the gossipy variety. It was a 'hilarious' joke played on customers across the drinking world with bartenders all in collusion. But what of his eponymous cocktail? It's as simple and infuriatingly fresh as the mystery man himself: gin, lemon juice, simple syrup and club soda, served over ice and gone in a flash.

1   Fill a Collins glass half to two-thirds with ice.

2   Shake the gin, simple syrup and lemon juice over ice.

3   Strain into the glass, add the soda and garnish with a lemon wheel.

SUNNY'S

Redhook, USA

Sunny's sits in the flat grid of streets at the edge of Brooklyn, in a neighbourhood of squat warehouses and hipster house shares and close to a famous three-level crab house (and an Ikea, if you're in the mood for Poang or a Lack). Outside, a vintage flatbed is parked, and when the sun sets, the water of Red Hook dock twinkles in the distance; you'll think it's the most beautifully appointed dive bar in the world.

Family owned since 1890 and apparently little changed since those early days, John's Restaurant and Bar (as Sunny's was known then) was once popular with longshoremen, but by the 1980s Red Hook had experienced the beginnings of a vibe shift, with a hipper, less nautical crowd moving to the neighbourhood, and the place called itself the Red Hook Yacht and Kayak Club. It was briefly closed in 2001 but relaunched soon after as the Sunny's we know and love today. Sunny's is packed with artifacts, ephemera and merchandise, and it is no stranger to the limelight. It's been visited by everyone from documentary crews to Anthony Bourdain and Lady Gaga (who performed there in 2016 as part of a live dive tour). There are seasonal art exhibitions, live music most nights with a penchant for bluegrass bands (including one standout, silver fox harmonica player), and a bright and tight cocktail menu that includes the Dark & Stormy, Old Fashioned and the Manhattan (fitting, as the city looms close on the horizon).

MARTINEZ

Glass	Serves	Karaoke Track
Coupe or Tumbler	1	'There's No One Quite Like Grandma' by St Winifred's School Choir

INGREDIENTS

60 ml (2 fl oz) London dry gin

20 ml (¾ fl oz) sweet vermouth

½ tbsp (¼ fl oz) cherry liqueur

2 dashes Angostura bitters

Classic ice cubes

Lemon twist

EQUIPMENT

Jigger

Mixing glass

Bar spoon

Cocktail strainer

If you believe what they say, you'll know the Martinez is the grandmother of another famous drink, the Martini. In fact, one couldn't exist without the other, much like Madonna and Gaga. To wear out the analogy, the Martinez is a little sweeter than its offspring, with its sweet vermouth and cherry liqueur.

Was it created in Martinez, California, as the city itself suggests? No one really knows, but the age of the recipe might be pinpointed to at least the late 1800s, when it appeared in famous bartender Jerry Thomas's book *The Bar-Tender's Guide* (1862). Thomas claimed he created the Martinez, but historians suggest the booze-star might have taken others' recipes and passed them off as his own (much like Gaga and – well, you get the picture). Either way, the Martinez is one of the oldest cocktails on the drinks list (just like – oh, you know).

1   Add the liquid ingredients to a mixing glass half full of ice and stir until frosty/you reach the edge of glory.

2   Strain into a coupe or tumbler.

3   Add a lemon twist to garnish and serve/express yourself.

21

WHISKY SOUR

Glass	Serves	Karaoke Track
Coupe or Old Fashioned	1	'Bootylicious' by Destiny's Child

INGREDIENTS

60 ml (2 fl oz) bourbon

20 ml (¾ fl oz) freshly squeezed lemon juice

15 ml (½ fl oz) simple syrup

15 ml (½ fl oz) fresh egg white (optional)

Classic ice cubes

Large ice cube

2 dashes Angostura bitters

Lemon twist

Maraschino cherries on a spear

EQUIPMENT

Jigger

Shaker

Cocktail strainer

Let's go back to 1862 and the Whisky Sour's first mention in print, as the stand out concoction of Jerry Thomas's *Bar-Tender's Guide*. Of course, there must have been similar sweet and sour ways of drinking the amber stuff in centuries past, but the Whisky Sour is the superior method. Once the province of monks who – miraculously – turned beer into whisky, the spirit was thought of as a cure-all and pick-me-up until its recreational powers became its point of interest. Now it's the must-have cocktail ingredient and we're all the better for it.

The question is: to egg or not to egg? The earliest recipes called for a little egg white, first shaken 'dry' without ice, then with ice, once the cocktail was properly mixed. The result is a velvety, creamy texture with a delightful amount of froth on top. Today the egg white trick has fallen somewhat out of fashion (and your local dive might not be the place to expect the freshest of eggs), but the original was firmly egg-conditional. Let's say the egg is optional and the real key is to achieve the Sour's delicate balance (hence why making your own in the early hours isn't advised; it's more an early evening drink). Much like Destiny's Child, the sweet simple syrup, cheek-caving sour citrus and the spiced warmth of bourbon all must sing with the same note.

1   Egg-lover? Shake the bourbon, lemon juice, simple syrup and egg white *without* ice – about 20 seconds should do it – then add ice and shake again until frosty. Strain into a chilled glass with a large cube of ice, add two dashes of bitters, a lemon wheel and cherries, and serve. Egg-fighter? Shake over ice, strain, add bitters and garnishes, and serve.

22

Boulevardier

Glass	Serves	Essential Snack
Coupe or Nick & Nora	1	British delicacy Twiglets or US-dream potato chip Ruffles

INGREDIENTS

40 ml (1¼ fl oz) bourbon or rye
30 ml (1 fl oz) Campari
30 ml (1 fl oz) sweet vermouth
Classic ice cubes
Large and unwieldly orange twist

EQUIPMENT

Jigger
Mixing glass
Bar spoon
Cocktail strainer

Behold, the greatest cocktail in the world (no questions will be taken at this time) and one of the easiest to mix. Greatness really shouldn't be this easy, but it is. The history of the Boulevardier (a sort of socialite) is as chic as anything. Erskine 'Foxy' Gwynne – the American publisher of *The Boulevardier* magazine, the late 1920s must-read tome for the upscale and English-speaking immigrant community in Paris – is the drink's creator. In fact, Harry MacElhone included the Boulevardier in his 1927 book *Barflies and Cocktails* and attributed it to Foxy.

A distant relation of the Vanderbilts, Foxy was a looker: a ripped blonde pocket-rocket who had already made headlines when he punched the lights out of a priggish fellow bad-mouthing a young woman at a posh party. Soon after, the young woman married Foxy, her avenger. Anything Foxy touched turned to gold, and it's little wonder his cocktail recipe endures. One sip of a Boulevardier and you'll be transported to the Roaring Twenties, all boozy parties, ballroom punch-ups, monied Parisian trendsetters and lines of 'naughty salt'. It's cool-fuel, so to speak.

The eagle-eyed might point out this chic whiskey, sweet vermouth and Campari concoction is like the Negroni, but while the gin-based 'Roni is like a fragrant slap in the face, the Boulevardier, leading with whiskey or rye, is rich and warm. Best served with Twiglets or Ruffles potato chips – if your drink's this classy, you'll be hankering for something filthy and basic to temper it with.

1 Add the bourbon or rye, Campari and sweet vermouth to a mixing glass and stir with ice until chilled.

2 Strain into a glass and serve with an annoyingly large orange twist.

23

VERMOUTH & TONIC

Glass	Serves	Essential Viewing
Highball	1	*Bridesmaids* (2011)

INGREDIENTS

Classic ice cubes
60 ml (2 fl oz) vermouth
Audaciously large
  citrus wedge
Chilled tonic water, to top

EQUIPMENT

Jigger

Vermouth: always the bridesmaid, playing second fiddle to more dominating, flashy spirits with their indisputable star power. But here she is, muscling in on aperitivo hour like some overlooked but delightful guest. 'Let's welcome Vermouth and her best buddy, Tonic!'

There are two main types of vermouth, dry and sweet, but all are welcome in this two-element drink. Simply add vermouth to tonic water with lots of ice and a massive piece of citrus and you'll never look at aperitivo hour the same way. Of course, mentioning aperitivo hour in a non-European dive bar might be met with eye rolls, but in its birthplace, Italy, it's a convivial drinking period based around delicious and salty dive-bar-oriented snacks (and who could quibble with that?). You might say that the US version, happy hour, is arguably a yearning to capture the boozy camaraderie inherent in Italian aperitivo hour, that golden, sunset sprawl onto sidewalks and under Campari umbrellas. Vermouth, the fortified wine indigenous to Italy (although other countries often claim to be its birthplace), is a quiet yet essential component in a host of classic cocktails, from the Martini to the Americano. Secondary flavours include rosso (red), bianco (a sort of dry-sweet fence-sitter), amber and rosé, but for almost all cocktails, dry, sweet and rosso are your go-tos. They won't let you down.

1   Add ice, vermouth and citrus wedge to a highball then top with chilled tonic water. *Perfezione.*

ESPRESSO MARTINI

Glass	Serves	Karaoke Track
Coupe or Martini	1	'Firestarter' by The Prodigy

INGREDIENTS

60 ml (2 fl oz) vodka
(Dick likes Wyborowa)

15 ml (½ fl oz) coffee liqueur
(Kahlúa ideally, who are
we kidding that there's
anything better?)

30 ml (1 fl oz) fresh espresso,
chilled, or cold brew

15 ml (½ fl oz) simple syrup

Classic ice cubes

3 'lucky' coffee beans

EQUIPMENT

Jigger

Shaker

Cocktail strainer

BARTENDER'S NOTE

Cooled and chilled espresso is
perfect if you don't have cold
brew; instant is a firm no.

Once thought to have been created by Satan himself, this devilishly sweet late-night cocktail – the fabled fire-starter of hard-to-forget adventures – was conjured by legendary barkeep Dick Bradsell during his late 1980s stint at Fred's Club in London. Dick encountered a young model (the identity of whom Dick will not reveal, only to say she is almost as famous as the drink in question) who asked for something that would both 'wake her up' and 'f**k her up'. Dick answered her poetic call with a little poetry of his own. And so, he changed both the cocktail world and bachelorette parties forever and created the Espresso Martini.

Dick's perfectly balanced recipe was a hit and – just like the magical effects it lends its drinkers – it had real staying power. It's not every day a one-off cocktail, created on the fly for a model in a darkened London club, becomes one of the world's most popular drinks, but Dick nailed it. Vodka, coffee liqueur, sugar syrup and a shot of fresh espresso or cold brew: guaranteed to wake you up and, well, you know the rest.

1   Shake vodka, coffee liqueur, chilled espresso or cold brew and simple syrup over ice until frosty.

2   Strain into a chilled coupe or Martini glass.

3   Add three coffee beans to garnish.

Dirty Martini

Glass	Serves	Karaoke Track
Coupe or Martini	1	'Dirrty' by Christina Aguilera

INGREDIENTS

Classic ice cubes

75 ml (2½ fl oz) vodka or gin

30 ml (1 fl oz) dry vermouth

15 ml (½ fl oz) olive brine, or to taste

2–3 olives

Classic ice cubes

EQUIPMENT

Mixing glass

Jigger

Bar spoon

Cocktail strainer

BARTENDER'S NOTE

If in doubt, try two parts gin or vodka, one-part dry vermouth and as much brine as you like.

So many of us always seem to take something perfect and then absolutely ruin it. Luckily, there's a drink for that. If you're at your local dive, quietly contemplating the self-imposed wreckage of your love life, career or finances, then the Dirty Martini is for you. It's a briny, savoury, put-hair-on-your-chest kind of drink; a classic Martini wrecked with olive (or sometimes caper) brine. Not-so-subtly powerful, it will take you just where you need to go: from maudlin mope at the bar to a slut-dropping Christina Aguilera wannabe from whose cold, vice-like grip the karaoke mic will have to be prised.

So, where did this magical recipe originate? Was it first mixed and sipped in the US in the early 1930s? The Dirty Martini's earliest mention in print is in G.H. Steele's *My New Cocktail Book* (1931) but it is often claimed a briny Martini muddled with olives was first served by Waldorf Astoria bartender John E O'Connor as early as 1901. Perhaps O'Connor had some issues to deal with and thought that muddying a perfectly good drink with brine would be a way through it. Whatever his approach, we should all be glad he dirtied the Martini.

1   Fill a mixing glass two-thirds full with ice.

2   Add vodka or gin, dry vermouth and brine, and stir until frosty (you can shake the Dirty Martini, but you will probably end up with a diluted drink full of ice chips).

3   Strain into a chilled coupe or Martini glass.

4   Add a couple of olives (on a spear if you're feeling fancy) and serve.

TRISHA'S

London,
UK

First, there is the mystery of this infamous late-night London bar's true name. Is it Trisha's? Some call it the Hideout . . . or perhaps it's the New Evaristo Club? Maybe it's best just to identify it: it's hidden behind a nondescript door on Greek Street, Soho, and you'll probably be tipsy when you first visit. A friend or lover will take you into their confidence, and you'll enter the idiosyncratic, basement space, finding it stuffed with posters of Italian pop stars, the Pope and early-hours drinkers, characters and celebs, grinning and slurping down their drinks at round tables.

Soho has long been London's boozy playground, from the drinking crisis of the 1600s, when most of the city seemed to be soaked in gin, beer and loose living, all the way through to the gangland vice of the 1950s and onwards. At around 80 years old, making it one of Soho's oldest still-open haunts, Trisha's seems the perfect dive bar to carry on the city's boozy legacy into the future. Owner Trish Bergonzi took over the venue in 2001 and still seems to charge retro prices (lifetime membership is just £10). Like many of the most excellent dive bars in the world, wandering into Trisha's feels like being invited inside someone's home; if you don't embarrass yourself too much before closing time, you might be invited back again.

26

PORN STAR MARTINI

Glass	Serves	Essential Viewing
Coupe or Martini (Shot Glass Optional)	1	Boogie Nights (1997)

INGREDIENTS

60 ml (2 fl oz) vanilla vodka

15 ml (½ fl oz) vanilla simple syrup

15 ml (½ fl oz) freshly squeezed lime juice

15 ml (½ fl oz) Passoã liqueur

15 ml (½ fl oz) passion fruit purée

Classic ice cube

30 ml (1 fl oz) chilled prosecco

½ fresh passion fruit

EQUIPMENT

Jigger

Shaker

Is there anything better than gathering your crew – be they gal pals, church wardens, probation officers or your local canasta group – for a night of fruity drinks and fun? But why is it that the fruitier the drink, the more eye-popping the name? Bartenders have kept us amused for decades with curious and, at times somewhat humiliating, cocktail names to liven up our night. Have you ever been sent to the bar to order Sex on the Beach? A Screaming Orgasm? Or the impossibly inappropriate Slow Comfortable Screw Up Against a Wall? And then there's the Porn Star Martini.

Douglas Ankrah – the bartender and creator of the Porn Star Martini – first mixed and served the passion fruit-powered cocktail at the Townhouse Bar in London in 2002. Ankrah thought the cringe-inducing name might be an ice-breaker, but little did he know that the PSM would take the cocktail world by storm. Soon, it was the go-to for rowdy nights out and is even rumoured to have been part of Prince William's wooing strategy when he met his future wife, Catherine.

There is something inherently dive-y about the Porn Star Martini. Is it the name – conjuring thoughts of frosted lipstick and ice cubes on the nips? Is it its association with fun and frolics? Or is it the PSM's hands-down delicious taste? Who can tell. Cocktail purists might note that it is not actually a Martini, but who cares? Ankrah added vanilla vodka to Passoã liqueur, passion fruit purée and used lime to (almost) cut through the sweetness. He topped it with chilled prosecco, and some bartenders like to add a shot glass of extra prosecco on the side, because why not?

1   Shake the vodka, simple syrup, lime juice, Passoã and purée in a shaker with ice until frosty.

2   Strain into a coupe, top with chilled prosecco and float a passion fruit half on top. Serve with a shot of prosecco if you're so inclined.

27

Jägerbomb

Glass	Serves	Essential Snack
Highball or Half Pint and Shot	1	Shawarma in Pita With Chilli Sauce, Garlic Sauce, Fries

INGREDIENTS

60 ml (2 fl oz) Jägermeister

⅔ can Red Bull, chilled

The J-Bomb is an extraordinary drink. A shot of Jägermeister dropped into a glass two-thirds full of Red Bull and sipped before heading over to the karaoke machine, pool table or oddly sticky leather banquette to press lips against lips until the lights go up.

An unlikely paring, in a way, the success of the Jägerbomb has perky marketing intern written all over it: it's the answer to 'how the heck are we going get this curious 1930s aniseed liqueur that tastes like cough syrup onto the back bar of every dive in the world?' Whoever thought up this ingenious concoction lit a fire that has burned brightly since the early 1990s. Red Bull, the world's first energy drink, seemed to draw inspiration from Krating Daeng, the Thai drink popular in the 1970s. Jägermeister is the German herbal, spiced and deliriously sweet liqueur that had a somewhat genteel, digestif reputation on its launch in 1934 . . . until it met Red Bull more than six decades later. There's a rumour that the Bomb itself was first concocted at Lake Tahoe, California, in the late 1990s, apparently at an infamous après ski dive bar where the Jägerbombs were lined up to get the party started – and that party is still going strong.

If the J-bomb is what starts the night off with a bang, then it's the kebab that brings it to a close. Any self-respecting student knows the meaty snack's magical powers at tempering hangovers. If you've eschewed all thought of the J-bomb from your mind, why not allow it back? It's the taste of youth, misspent or otherwise.

1   Fill a highball or half pint two-thirds full with chilled Red Bull.

2   Serve with a shot of Jägermeister. Drop the shot glass into the Red Bull and guzzle down.

28

MAN ABOUT TOWN

Glass	*Serves*	*Karaoke Track*
Coupe	1	'I'm Waiting For the Man' by Nico and The Velvet Underground

INGREDIENTS

Classic ice cubes
90 ml (3 fl oz) rye whiskey
45 ml (1½ fl oz) sweet vermouth
45 ml (1½ fl oz) Cynar
Maraschino cherry

EQUIPMENT

Jigger
Mixing glass
Bar spoon
Cocktail strainer

It's time to pull up a slightly sticky bar stool and get to know the Man About Town, your new, worldly-wise, complicated and slightly bitter best bar-friend. Much like the Boulevardier is a twist on a Negroni, the Man About Town is a twist on a twist of a Negroni, if you will. Its magical three ingredients – spicy rye whiskey, sweet red vermouth and Sicilian bitters, Cynar – are certainly reminiscent of the Negroni, but the Man has a darker, more complex and surprisingly herbal taste.

Apparently we can thank much-loved NYC restaurant Gramercy Tavern for creating the Man in question. The Tavern – known for its endless list of awards and Michelin recognition – is hardly a dive bar, but nevertheless the MAT has that downbeat, mysterious vibe that feels more stuck to your seat than upscale eats. And isn't that just what we all need sometimes? The Man About Town is less Mr Right, more Mr Right Now.

1   First fill your coupe with ice.

2   Add the liquids, then the ice to a mixing glass and stir briskly for 20 seconds.

3   Discard the ice from the coupe, strain in the cocktail, add the cherry and you're all set to meet the man of your dreams.

29
NYC SOUR

Glass	Serves	Karaoke Track
Coupe or Tumbler	1	'Empire State of Mind' by Jay-Z feat. Alicia Keys

INGREDIENTS

Classic ice cubes

60 ml (2 fl oz) bourbon

30 ml (1 fl oz) lemon juice, freshly squeezed

30 ml (1 fl oz) pinot noir or a similarly light red wine

15 ml (½ fl oz) simple syrup

15 ml (½ fl oz) egg white or aquafaba (optional)

1 dash Angostura bitters

Lemon twist

EQUIPMENT

Jigger

Shaker

Cocktail strainer

New York City, arguably the home of the modern dive bar, is a place that likes to do things its own way. That's why there's no dithering in the deli, a bank-breaking 25% tip on a bottle of water and endless lines down the street for the latest 'it'-bake. The Whisky Sour is no exception, and the classic recipe has been tweaked to underline New York's point of difference. Enter the New York Sour, powered by bourbon, soft pinot noir and a sharp edge of citrus. Two contrasting tones (warm orange, ruby red) make it pleasingly showy, slightly dirty, as well as surprisingly delightful. Just like New York City itself.

1   First fill your coupe with ice.

2   Add the bourbon, lemon juice and simple syrup to a shaker.

3   If using egg white or aquafaba, add it now and shake 'dry' (without ice) for 20 seconds, then add ice and shake again. If not, add ice and shake until frosty.

4   Discard the ice from the coupe, strain the cocktail into the glass, then very slowly pour in the wine. Add a dash of bitters and lemon twist and serve.

30

HOT APPLE CIDER

Glass	Serves	Essential Bar Wear
Heatproof Glass Mug	4	Fur-lined Birkenstocks

INGREDIENTS

2–3 cinnamon sticks

6 cloves

6 allspice berries

1 orange peel, in strips

1 lemon peel, in strips

1.5 l (48 fl oz) cloudy apple juice

Juice of 1 lemon, freshly squeezed

60 ml (2 fl oz) dark maple syrup

180 ml (6 fl oz) spiced rum

Apple slices

EQUIPMENT

Jigger

Cheesecloth

Stainless-steel pan

If you like your hot drinks to have the intoxicating fragrance of a discount store autumnal candle (and really, who doesn't?) then US dive bar favourite Hot Apple Cider is for you. As soon as the crisp autumn weather appears, this delicious drink takes its place. Steaming, and possibly fermenting for an undisclosed number of hours, Hot Apple Cider fills the bar with the scent of cinnamon, clove and apple – and the anticipation of cosy knits, log fires and pumpkin-spiced everything. And if your local dive is worth its salted pretzels, a shot of spiced rum will be added to every order; it turns this heady concoction into something truly warming and wonderous.

1   Wrap up the spices and strips of citrus peel in a handkerchief-sized piece of cheesecloth and knot together to make a pouch.

2   Add the pouch to a saucepan with the apple juice, lemon juice and maple syrup. Warm over a low heat for 10 minutes or so until steaming (but not boiling).

3   Add a shot of spiced rum to each glass and top with the hot apple cider.

4   Add a fresh apple slice to garnish, then slip on a pair of fur-lined Birkenstock's and let it all go.

31

Glögg

Glass	Serves	Essential Bar Snack
Heatproof Glass Mug	4	Meatballs and Lingonberry Jam

INGREDIENTS

2–3 cinnamon sticks

6 cloves

6 cardamon pods, broken open

Thumb-sized piece of fresh ginger, peeled

1 bottle of light red wine

250 ml (8 fl oz) vodka

250 ml (8 fl oz) ruby port

1 cup light brown sugar

1 cup blanched whole almonds

1 cup raisins

Zest of an orange

EQUIPMENT

Cheesecloth

Stainless-steel pan

BARTENDER'S NOTE

Alternativley, you can add the cinnamon, cloves, cardamom and ginger to the vodka and leave to infuse for 24 hours at room temperature. Strain and add to the saucepan with the wine, port, sugar, almonds, zest and raisins. Warm over a low heat for 10 minutes, then serve.

Many of us only know Sweden, the belle of the Scandinavian Peninsula, through its incredibly successful soft diplomacy project Ikea. The furniture and meatball megastore, with branches in 31 countries around the world, is designed to spread Swedish cultural influence through its clever shelving systems, tea lights, lingonberry jam – and *glögg*, the delicious Swedish winter drink. In Ikea's famous food department, bottles of this sort-of mulled cordial are sold, ready to be mixed with a cheap cabernet sauvignon to make *glögg*, like mulled wine but with a pair of very big *balle*.

A mainstay of every Swedish Christmas house party, *glögg* also has a home in the dive bars of this land of liquorice chocolate and harsh winters, where seasoned drinkers insist on sipping it to an ABBA soundtrack. The addition of almonds and raisins can divide *glögg* fans – some like these chewy additions, others like their *glögg* strained and simple.

1 Wrap up the cinnamon, cloves, cardamom and ginger in a handkerchief-size piece of cheesecloth and knot together to make a pouch.

2 Add to a saucepan with the wine, vodka, port, sugar, almonds, raisins and zest. Warm over a low heat for 10 minutes or so until steaming (but not boiling).

3 Ladle into each mug – with a few of the almonds and raisins – and serve with a meatball on the side.

THE BEARDED TIT

Redfern,
Australia

Welcome to the Bearded Tit, the queerest dive bar in Sydney – quite the claim considering the city's famously LGBTQ+-friendly vibe. The Tit describes itself as 'part neighbourhood queer bar, gallery, and creative space' and 'local clubhouse for the parched, hungry, and curious', but its most endearing quality is that it doesn't take itself too seriously.

Founded by Joy Ng in 2014, the Tit has become the last word in queer acceptance, cold beer and hot pies. Step beyond the taxidermy deer bums and crochet dildos (the Tit is famous for its salty artworks), underwear parties, eye-popping performances and Tit Talks, and you'll find that rarest of things: a really good pub.

There are draught beers and cans, great cocktails (from Dark & Stormys and Martinis to a house special, Two in the Pink), retro cheese and charcuterie plates, beige snacks in baskets, and the Titters do a famous Triple-Hot Sauce Bloody Mary that'll blow your head off. There are sometimes-changing collections of merchandise (a dive bar essential), with a focus on racy t-shirt prints. Plus there's the traditional pub interior and a delightful beer garden with a caravan to smooch in. *Viva la Tit*!

32

MICHELADA

Glass	Serves	Karaoke Track
Pint Glass or Pint Mug	1	'La Bamba' by Ritchie Valens

INGREDIENTS

2 tsp Kosher or flaked salt

2 tsp Tajín powder, plus an extra pinch

60 ml (2 fl oz) fresh lime juice

Classic ice cubes

5 drops hot sauce, such as Tabasco

2 drops Worcestershire sauce

2 drops soy sauce or Maggi Sauce Seasoning

180 ml (6 fl oz) tomato juice, or clamato

Lime wedges

1 bottle of light Mexican beer

EQUIPMENT

Saucer for rimming

Brunch: a time for gossip, hollandaise and impossibly stressful no-reservations situations. If you can survive the morning waiting two hours for a table, navigating steely eyed hostesses, screaming hoards high on Mimosas and undercooked corn fritters, you might want to continue the festivities at your local dive bar, where life is less . . . high stakes. And whatever you started with a Bloody Mary, the Michelada will finish. In fact, think of the Michelada – the jewel of the Mexican day-drinking scene – as the lighter, more fun cousin of the Bloody Mary. But where the Mary can become overwrought and idiosyncratic with its Italian caper berries, freshly grated organic horseradish and vegan bacon bits, the Michelada is all confident simplicity. In essence, it's a beer cocktail with tomato juice, lime, hot sauce and spices, and it's delicious.

1   Mix the salt and Tajín (a tangy, citrusy and slightly spicy seasoning mix) in a saucer, moisten the rim of a chilled glass with lime juice and dip to rim.

2   Build the drink with ice (about a third full), seasonings (hot sauce, Worcestershire, soy or Maggi, and another pinch of Tajín), then add the tomato or clamato juice, lime wedge and top with chilled Mexican beer.

Shandy

Glass	Serves	Essential Vape Flavour
Pint Glass or Pint Mug	1	Strawberries and Cream

INGREDIENTS

Individual bottle of lemon soda

Bottle or can of lager, pale ale or bitter

The mildly alcoholic drink of beer and fizzy lemonade beloved by the Brits is traditionally drunk all summer long in pub beer gardens, through swarms of wasps, clouds of barbecue smoke and dessert-flavoured vape. It is so ubiquitous that, left unguarded on picnic tables in the summer sun, it's the golden booze many admit to first trying as a child. In fact, in the 1970s and '80s – problematic but probably more fun times – UK children's soda brands Top Deck and Shandy Bass were made with real beer and a little alcohol too. In this way it is the gateway drink; look up and down any dive bar and the be-stooled clientele will no doubt have started with something as innocent as a Shandy. The original 1850s Shandy, the Shandygaff, was a delicious mix of beer and ginger ale – reputedly a favourite of Charles Dickens. But it's the contemporary version that's the most delicious. A 50/50 mix of chilled lager (a pale ale or bitter works well too) and lemonade (carbonated, not the flat kind) makes the perfect drink. In Germany it's called the Radler, i.e. 'cyclist', in honour of beer lovers who have to take the road at the end of the afternoon, and the Mexican Chelada (a glug of fresh lime juice, salted rim on the glass, chilled beer) is arguably the Shandy's distant cousin.

1   Fill the glass half full of lemonade, then slowly pour in the beer down the side of the glass and serve with classic British pub snacks: crisps (chips), Frazzles (bacon-flavoured corn snacks), and/or Scampi Fries (hugely divisive and heavily fragranced shrimp-flavoured snacks). Whip out a fully charged vape like a true Brit and wile away the afternoon until golden hour.

YALE COCKTAIL

Glass	*Serves*	*Entry Requirements*
Coupe or Martini	1	A 4.0 GPA and the Unrivalled Privilege of Old Money

INGREDIENTS

45 ml (1½ fl oz) gin
20 ml (¾ fl oz) dry vermouth
1 tsp Blue Curaçao
Dash of Peychaud's Bitters
Classic ice cubes

EQUIPMENT

Jigger
Mixing glass
Bar spoon
Cocktail strainer

In 1980, legendary tome *The Official Preppy Handbook* was published. Lisa Birnbach's legendary comic celebration (or was it take-down?) of American Ivy league culture skewered the unknowingly privileged lives and style of those refined college kids – who then went on to rule the world. *The Handbook* – a masterpiece, truth be told – inspired *Tipsy in Madras* (2004) a celebration of cocktails beloved by the preppy masses. Its push to go back to the '80s for cocktail inspiration is one this book can get behind. Those Ivy League cocktails (the colleges almost all have their own unofficial concoction) are as garish as they are delicious – and, yes, have that dive bar quality (the preppies love slumming it in Daddy's rugby shirt). The Yale is one such drink, dating back to the 1800s, and is thought to have been devised in the bar-land of New York. It's a Martini-style drink and as blue as a 1980s freshman's favourite movie genre.

1   Stir the ingredients over ice and strain into a chilled coupe or Martini glass. The Peychaud's lends a little fruity spice and the Blue Curaçao is an essential nod to the Yale school colours.

35

ROB ROY

Glass	*Serves*	*Essential Bar Snack*
Nick & Nora or Coupe	1	Deep-Fried Mars Bar

INGREDIENTS

60 ml (2 fl oz) premium Scotch whisky

20 ml (¾ fl oz) sweet vermouth

3 dashes of Angostura bitters

Classic ice cubes

3 brandied cherries on a spear

EQUIPMENT

Jigger

Mixing glass

Cocktail strainer

Bar spoon

Visit a lively Glasgow dive bar and you're unlikely to find the rather refined Rob Roy and probably more likely to discover vodka mixed with the nation's bright orange soda, Irn-Bru, with a side of pickled eggs and the culinary masterpiece that is the deep-fried chocolate bar. Rob Roy is the proudly Scottish version of the Manhattan that swaps in blended Scotch whisky, Italian vermouth and aromatic bitters. It's not a great leap from the bourbon-centred Manhattan itself, but using Scotch gives the drink a point of difference – and a little Scottish fire in your belly. It's a smoky, warming recipe with a theatrical past. Created at the Waldorf Astoria in 1897, the Rob Roy is said to have been inspired by the operetta *Rob Roy*, performed at the Herald Square Theatre nearby, all about the Scottish Robin Hood.

If an operetta-inspired cocktail doesn't feel like the drink you might confidently order at a Glasgow dive, you'll need to double your haggis intake: the Roy needs to take its rightful place as Scotland's national drink. If mixing at home, use your favourite premium Scotch whisky – there's no place to hide in such a simple, confident recipe.

1   Stir the ingredients over ice and strain into a chilled Nick & Nora or coupe.

2   Garnish with brandied cherries on a spear.

36
OYSTER BAY

Glass	Serves	Essential Bar Snack
Coupe	1	Pickled Oyster-Flavoured Corn Snacks

INGREDIENTS

Classic ice cubes

60 ml (2 fl oz) premium Scotch whisky

10 ml (⅓ fl oz) Noilly Prat Extra Dry vermouth

10 ml (⅓ fl oz) orange curaçao liqueur

1 tsp freshly squeezed lemon juice

Dash of orange bitters

EQUIPMENT

Jigger

Mixing glass

Bar spoon

Cocktail strainer

BARTENDER'S NOTE

Some recipes require the maker to strain the lemon juice so the cocktail is completely clear, but who has time for that? Oyster makers: you do you.

There are many bays to celebrate, from Copacabana to Michael, but the often-over-looked Oyster Bay is worthy of praise too. This delicious drink has earned itself two seeming inspirations: the first is its curious colour, which is indeed oyster-like – a fleshy, orange-tinged drop that looks a little like dive-bar dishwater (but, thankfully, that's where the similarity ends). The other inspiration is that its name is thought to be derived from the New York State hometown of one Theodore Roosevelt: teddy bear collector, tree hugger, grad college dropout and president. Whatever the Bay's true history, it's a cocktail-counter stalwart for a reason. Scotch whisky, extra-dry French vermouth, a little orange curaçao and citrus makes up the Oyster Bay's unique flavour profile, smokier and hardier than sweet and easy. And the lily-livered needn't be queasy: there is no fresh or pickled oyster lurking at the bottom of the Oyster Bay, only the brilliant idea to order one more.

1 Stir the ingredients over ice and strain into a chilled coupe.

37

7 & 7

Glass	Serves	Karaoke Track
Tumbler or Highball	1	'Here You Come Again' by Dolly Parton

INGREDIENTS

2 shots (2 fl oz) Seagram's
   7 Crown whiskey

Classic ice cubes

7-Up, chilled, to top

EQUIPMENT

Jigger

BARTENDER'S NOTE

Variations are not allowed. But might you add a dash of orange bitters to upgrade the citrus taste? Sure, just tell no one.

Second only to the Shot & Beer, in the Americas you would be hard pushed to find a more dive-y drink order than a Seagram's 7 Crown and 7-Up combo. Affectionately called 7 & 7, it is one of the easiest two-parters known to bartenders everywhere. With a history spanning back to the 1930s, post-Prohibition times, Seagram's 7 Crown Whiskey was once arguably the most dominant and revered drop in Canada and the States, and mixed with lemon-and-lime soda, 7-Up, became the go-to way to drink it. In recent decades the 7 Crown's fame waned as drinkers were lured toward the clear stuff: vodka, gin and tequila.

As whiskey seems to be making something of a comeback, 7 Crown is back on the lips of dive drinkers across the American continent, and so too is the 7 & 7. In fact, Seagram's owners, Diageo, pushed the 7 & 7 as the quintessential dive bar drink in their 2018 ad campaign, calling for drinkers to return to their favourite dives. And, sure enough, they did.

Making a 7 & 7 at home is a cinch: one sip and you will be transported to the perfect dive bar, with sailors on leave, stale potato chips in bamboo bowls, someone's dog padding about, and Dolly cranking out of the jukebox: 7th heaven.

1   Add ice and whiskey to a glass.

2   Top with chilled 7-Up, and serve.

38

La Louisiane

Glass	Serves	Essential Reading
Coupe or Old Fashioned	1	*Drawing Blood* by Poppy Z. Brite

INGREDIENTS

90 ml (3 fl oz) rye whisky
20 ml (¾ fl oz) sweet vermouth
15 ml (½ fl oz) Benedictine
2–3 dashes of Absinthe
2–3 dashes of Peychaud's Bitters
Classic ice cubes
Huge single cube (optional)
Brandied cherry on a spear

EQUIPMENT

Jigger
Mixing glass
Bar spoon
Cocktail strainer

Let's head to New Orleans, a city steeped in history, from early Vodou temples to horror writer Poppy Z. Brite's absinthe-drinking goth vampires of the 1990s, to the modern Mardi Gras celebrations and boozy mishaps of Malcolm D. Lee's *Girls Trip* (2017). Cocktails are the lifeblood of New Orleans, and La Louisiane is a home-grown wonder. If you're butch enough for a Manhattan, you will know how to handle Louisiane – one of those brisk, puts-hair-on-your-chest cocktails with its spicy, darkly herbal and spooky edge. Instead of the Manhattan's bourbon, La Louisiane asks for the heat of a spicy rye whiskey, Benedictine (an oddly delicious bitter digestif with a cough-syrup taste) and a little sweet vermouth for balance.

The recipe is the onetime house drink of New Orleans' restaurant La Louisiane, which has been proudly standing and serving since 1881, and is itself a variation on the Vieux Carré (which is too heady even for this book). Cocktail-maker Jeffrey Morgenthaler's own delicious variation, the Sore Loser, uses bourbon, crème de pêche and sherry, but let's stick to the classic here, with its absinthe aroma.

1   Stir the liquid ingredients with ice.

2   Strain into a chilled coupe, or present in an Old Fashioned glass with a single mega ice cube.

3   Garnish with a brandied cherry on a spear.

39

GIN, GRAPEFRUIT *and* BITTERS

Glass	*Serves*	*Essential Snack*
Highball	1	Salted Pretzels

INGREDIENTS

Classic ice cubes

90 ml (3 fl oz) gin

180 ml (6 fl oz) freshly
squeezed grapefruit juice

3 or more dashes
of Angostura bitters

Huge grapefruit twist

1 small can of Schweppes
tonic water, chilled, to top

EQUIPMENT

Jigger

There are so many ways to drink gin and the British have perfected all its iterations, from the booze-loving Bright Young Things in the 1930s to the young Queen Mum in the 1950s, but by the '60s the clear stuff had fallen out of favour. Discovering new mixers and recipes – and an explosion of new craft distilleries – dragged it back into contemporary consciousness. One such drink is the simple yet startling Gin, Grapefruit and Bitters. A version of the British pub Gin and Bitter Lemon (a bitter, cloudy lemon soda) – a go-to for gin fans until the early 1990s – the Gin, Grapefruit and Bitters is the perfect drop. Go fresh and pink with your grapefruit, the spirit's true citrus companion. Lots of ice (this one needs to be painfully cold) and heavy on the bitters lifts this drink to another level.

1   Build in a chilled glass half full of ice cubes, add the gin, grapefruit and bitters, slip in the twist and top with chilled tonic water.

40

AMARETTO SOUR

Glass	Serves	Karaoke Track
Coupe	1	'Nasty' by Janet Jackson

INGREDIENTS

90 ml (3 fl oz) Amaretto

30 ml (1 fl oz) freshly squeezed lemon juice

30 ml (1 fl oz) simple syrup

15 ml (½ fl oz) egg white (optional)

1 tbsp bourbon

Classic ice cubes

Lemon twist

Brandied cherries

EQUIPMENT

Jigger

Shaker

Cocktail strainer

Much like Spam fondue, Fresca and cheese logs, Amaretto is the taste of the 1970s. The painfully sweet Italian almond or apricot-stone liqueur has the dark red-brown hue of whisky with the heady aroma of marzipan – it's like drinking a liquidised Christmas cake. A simple two-parter, the Amaretto Sour was the go-to way to drink it: Amaretto and freshly squeezed lemon juice to balance the sweet, with or without a little egg white for a velvety mouthfeel. But in recent years a little bourbon has been added to the mix, rounding out the Amaretto flavour, and the retro cocktail has been somewhat rediscovered. As ever, the egg white is optional, but be brave and go for it.

1 If using the egg white, dry shake the liquids without ice for 15 seconds.

2 Add ice and shake (again) until frosty.

3 Strain into a coupe glass, add garnishes and serve. Cheese log optional but recommended.

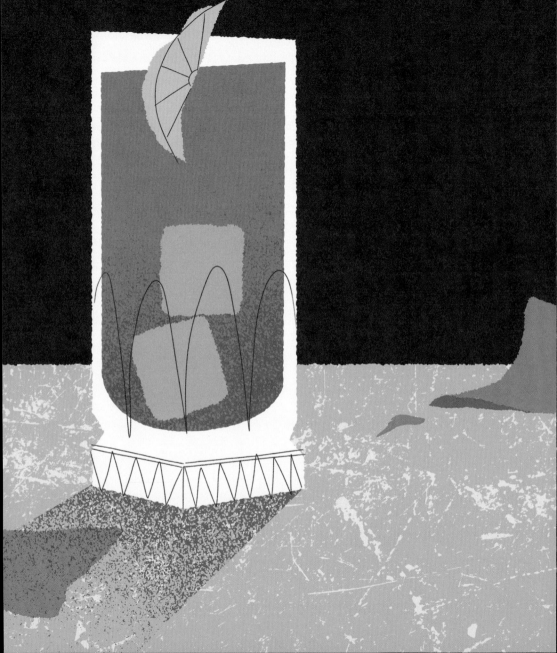

41

Pink Gin and Tonic

Glass	Serves	Karaoke Track
Highball	1	'Raise Your Glass' by P!NK

INGREDIENTS

Classic ice cubes
90 ml (3 fl oz) gin
Chilled tonic water, to top
15 ml (½ fl oz) cassis

EQUIPMENT

Jigger

It's hard to improve on the holy union of the gin and tonic, but this recipe – with its delicate pink hue and light berry flavour – turns the thoughtful, chic mixer drink into a teenage alcopop . . . and it's all the better for it. Any crème de cassis or crème de mûre can be used here – both dark berry-flavoured liqueurs usually saved for Kirs and Kir Royales, but they are the perfect sweetener in gin recipes. Simply build a classic gin and tonic with lots of ice, lime wedge, add in a little cassis, and get into the pink.

1 Build in the glass, drop in the cassis and sip (with your little finger stuck out for added refinement).

42

COLD BREW SPRITZER

Glass	Serves	Karaoke Track
Old Fashioned	1	'Coffee & TV' by Blur

INGREDIENTS

120 ml (4 fl oz) cold brew, chilled

120 ml (4 fl oz) tonic water, chilled

45 ml (1½ fl oz) vodka (optional)

Dash of freshly squeezed lemon juice

Large ice cube

Lemon twist

EQUIPMENT

Jigger

Kermit and Miss Piggy, Sia and Pitbull, Dua and Elton . . . sometimes the oddest bedfellows turn out to be the most intriguing pairings. And so it is with cold brew coffee and tonic. It's the fizzy, caffeinated energy drink that feels so much classier than Monster or Red Bull – even if you're using the dregs of the coffee pot.

We can thank the Swedes for this gift, especially those at Koppi Roasters Café in Helsingborg. Their espresso tonic was the result of boozy experimentation at a staff party back in 2007, and the accidental recipe soon made it onto Koppi's official menu and has since fizzed its way around the world.

The recipe calls for roughly half and half cold brew and tonic, with a squeeze of lemon, and lots of ice. A shot of Swedish vodka is optional but encouraged.

1   Build in the glass with a large ice cube.

2   Garnish with a lemon twist.

TWO SCHMUCKS

Barcelona, Spain

Meet Moe Aljaff and AJ White, two utter schmucks and the founders of Barcelona's best dive bar in the historic and delightfully scruffy El Raval district. Inside, the bar – a one-time taco eatery, deliriously haphazard in décor – is underpinned by an off-white tiled bar back; it's a gorgeous space, airier and brighter than the average dive. Impressively, Aljaff and White built the tiny bar interior by hand and described it as a 'five-star dive bar' to the press fascinated by this cooler-than-anything hangout.

When White moved on, Aljaff seemed intent on taking over the neighbourhood, opening two new venues on the same street: a comfort-food restaurant called Fat Schmuck and a late-night party bar called Lucky Schmuck. In fact, the Schmucks are schmucking even further with pop-ups in existing bars around the world.

In 2021, Aljaff handed over the keys to the original bar to another couple of schmucks, Parisian bar stars Pom Modeste and Juliette Larrouy, who have been tasked with keeping Schmucks' well-earned place in the 50 Best Bars in the World list. One thing is certain, Modeste and Larrouy have stayed true to the venue's original promise: to be a dive bar in all senses of the word, except when it comes to the quality and creativity of the drinks. Then, it's quite a serious affair.

43

OLD PAL

Glass	Serves	Karaoke Track
Martini	1	'Thank You For Being a Friend' by Andrew Gold

INGREDIENTS

60 ml (2 fl oz) rye whiskey

60 ml (2 fl oz) Campari

60 ml (2 fl oz) dry French vermouth

Classic ice cubes

Lemon twist

EQUIPMENT

Jigger

Mixing glass

Bar spoon

Cocktail strainer

Friends: you can't live with them. Well, at least you shouldn't unless you really must – who wants to fall out over toilet paper misuse or accidently sleeping with someone's ex? But if *The Golden Girls* have taught us anything, there is something magical about the most enduring friendships, from the delicious shorthand you might share to the slow pleasure of growing old together and pigging out on cheesecake. Luckily, there's a drink for that: the Old Pal.

Like the Boulevardier, the Old Pal is a twist on the Negroni but with spicy rye whiskey (when the Negroni would use gin), dry French vermouth (sweet is used in the Negroni) and Campari. Some claim the Boulevardier and Old Pal are, in fact, old pals themselves, both originating in the American ex-pat community in 1920s Paris. But the Old Pal does have a point of difference: it seems lighter and brighter than the Boulevardier. An uncomplicated old pal – what could be more delightful than that?

1 Stir the liquid ingredients with ice, strain and serve in a chilled Martini glass.

2 Garnish with a lemon twist.

44

NEGRONI SBAGLIATO
with PROSECCO

Glass	Serves	Essential Viewing
Tumbler	1	HBO's *House of the Dragon*, Season 1

INGREDIENTS

Classic ice cubes
45 ml (1½ fl oz) sweet vermouth
45 ml (1½ fl oz) Campari
Chilled prosecco, to top

EQUIPMENT

Jigger

Cast your mind back to September 2022 and a world-stopping media event: the dropping of HBO's cute 'getting to know you' TikTok feature of a Q&A with Olivia Cooke and Emma D'Arcy, the young British stars of the *Game of Thrones* prequel *House of the Dragon*. As is the case with all internet phenomena, the video went viral for almost no reason at all. It was the charming way Emma D'Arcy described their favourite drink: 'Negroni. Sbagliato. With prosecco in it.' The moment was memed into being, copied countless times and no doubt had real world consequences: a huge spike in Negroni Sbagliato sales.

The Negroni is made from gin, Campari and sweet vermouth, but in the case of the Sbagliato, the gin is 'forgotten' and prosecco is added instead. Luckily D'Arcy's favoured drink is delicious: both sweet and bitter with a head set of bubbles. Part of the charm of the clip – and the drink – is D'Arcy's cute delivery, their chemistry with Cooke and the fact that D'Arcy is non-binary, hence the meme's particular appeal with extremely online LGBTQ+ people. At the time of writing, the original clip has been viewed more than 10 million times: that's a lot of extra Sbagliatos and tipsy LGBTQ+ folk.

1 Build in a tumbler with ice, top with prosecco, post on TikTok immediately.

45

SALTY DOG

Glass	Serves	Essential Snacks
Highball	1	Dog Biscuits

INGREDIENTS

Flaked salt for rimming
45 ml (1½ fl oz) vodka or gin
Classic ice cubes
90 ml (3 fl oz) freshly
  squeezed grapefruit juice
Grapefruit twist

EQUIPMENT

Saucer
Jigger

In the United Kingdom, a dog in a pub is a truly comforting sight: it means all is well with the world. Be it a softly farting golden Labrador, a hyperactive Doodle, or an angry Jack Russell eating crisps under a table, dogs are not just tolerated, they are celebrated. But other great nations tend to avoid this canine free-for-all. In New York City, for example, dogs are rarely allowed access to anywhere that serves food (citing something to do with health and safety), putting most cafés, restaurants and dive bars out of reach. That doesn't stop the most hardened of dog owners, though, and many a Shiba Inu is snuck inside to nod along to LeAnn Rimes and be fed pretzel crumbs. Failing that, the Salty Dog is a perfect substitute. A classic recipe hailing from the 1950s, it's almost a Greyhound (the original gin and juice) but with a savoury, salted rim that gives it a strong point of difference. Like most two-ingredient drinks, the quality of the spirit and juice should be just so – and the whole drink should be incredibly well chilled – and all will be well with the world.

1   Moisten the rim of a highball and dip into a saucer of salt.

2   Build with the spirit, a generous serving of ice and top with grapefruit juice and a twist. That's a good boy.

46
Tequila Sunrise

Glass	*Serves*	*Karaoke Track*
Highball	1	'Sunrise, Sunset' by Perry Como

INGREDIENTS

Classic ice cubes

45 ml (2 fl oz) tequila

120 ml (4 fl oz) freshly squeezed orange juice, chilled

15 ml (½ fl oz) grenadine

Orange wheel

Maraschino cherries on a spear

EQUIPMENT

Jigger

Straw

This is the taste of the 1970s and '80s, evoking motel bars, frosted lipstick, dubious dive-bar bathrooms and a steamy 1988 crime romcom with Michelle Pfeiffer, Mel Gibson and Kurt Russell. The Tequila Sunrise is an essential part of cocktail history, even if most modern bartenders are sniffy about it. It's tart, refreshing and sweet, and the colours – bright, lurid – are more nuclear sunset than tequila, but isn't that twice the charm?

The Tequila Sunrise is thought to have been created in Mexico during American Prohibition, when rich drinkers would have to travel south to get buzzed. It was known as 'a favourite in Tijuana' and its yellow-orange-ruby-red ombré tones gave the Sunrise a glamourous, eye-catching appeal. The trick here is to use quality ingredients: the freshest freshly squeezed orange juice, the smoothest tequila, the gourmet-est grenadine. A few of these and you'll be watching the sun rise in no time.

1   Fill your highball two-thirds full with ice.

2   Add tequila and orange juice.

3   Tilt the glass and slow pour the grenadine so it sinks to the bottom.

4   Garnish with the orange wheel and cherries and serve with a straw.

CANDLELIGHT LOUNGE

NEW ORLEANS, USA

CANDLE LIGHT

LOUNGE

Welcome to the Candlelight, an unassuming, painted yellow single-storey dive bar in Treme, New Orleans, and an integral part of jazz history, the legacy of Black musicians and a refuge for live music during the aftermath of Hurricane Katrina. For such a tiny venue, its cultural and community significance is immense.

When uncovering the true character of a particular neighbourhood, dive bars can often be overlooked. But in so many ways they are de facto community centres, and it seems the Candlelight Lounge was always thought of as this. Its founder, Leona Grandison, took over the venue in 1985 and immediately made it a welcoming second home for musicians and local social groups. Brass players would play regularly, some bands were 'based' at the Candlelight and the venue was soon known for showcasing the best brass talent the US had to offer.

Once known as the Grease Lounge, itself a popular music venue, the Candlelight has a rich history. It became – and still is – a popular stop-off point for Sunday second-line parades, those strutting brass band players for which New Orleans is so famous. There's live music most nights, with bands cranking out four- to six-hour sets, and the drinks are pleasingly dive-priced. But the Candlelight's most important accolade is that it survived Katrina and was an important part in preserving the history of Black live music.

47

PALOMA

Glass	Serves	Essential Bar Soundtrack
Coupe	1	'Spanish Flea' by Herb Alpert & The Tijuana Brass

INGREDIENTS

60 ml (2 fl oz) reposado tequila

Juice of ½ ruby grapefruit, freshly squeezed

15 ml (½ fl oz) lime juice, freshly squeezed

15 ml (½ fl oz) agave syrup (or simple syrup)

Classic ice cubes

60 ml (2 fl oz) soda water, chilled

Lime wheel

EQUIPMENT

Jigger

Shaker

Cocktail strainer

Have a love/hate relationship with tequila? The world's most divisive spirit can indeed make all your dreams or nightmares come true, and after overindulging some brave souls are left hastily married, tattooed or suffering a form of PTSD (Post-Tequila Stress Disorder). Lucky, then, the Paloma is a fresh, zingy and completely unique way of drinking tequila. This long drink, topped with chilled soda water, uses reposado as its base, pepped up with ruby grapefruit and lime.

1   Shake the tequila, juices and syrup over ice.

2   Strain into a chilled coupe.

3   Top with chilled soda and garnish with a lime wheel.

48

ACAPULCO

Glass	Serves	Essential Bar Wear
Tumbler	1	Budgie Smugglers

INGREDIENTS

30 ml (1 fl oz) reposado tequila

45 ml (1½ fl oz) white rum

45 ml (1½ fl oz) pink grapefruit juice

90 ml (3 fl oz) pineapple juice

15 ml (½ fl oz) simple syrup

15 ml (½ fl oz) egg white (optional)

Classic ice cubes

Maraschino cherries on a spear

Pineapple wedge

EQUIPMENT

Jigger

Shaker

Cocktail strainer

Slip into your sliders and skimpiest swim briefs and head down to shimmering Acapulco de Juárez beach – if only in your mind – as it's the inspiration behind this perfectly balanced tequila, rum and fruit juice cocktail. The 'Pulco leans toward the sour end of the spectrum, with a dry, slightly sharp taste.

1 Dry shake the liquid ingredients – if using egg white – without ice for 15 seconds.

2 Then add ice and shake again until frosty. Strain into an ice-filled tumbler.

3 Garnish with cherries and pineapple. Pull up your beach briefs and let the Acapulco take you somewhere tropical.

LAGERITA

Glass	Serves	Essential Bar Snack
Beer	1	Lunchtime Deli Sandwich

INGREDIENTS

1 lime

Flaked salt

60 ml (2 fl oz) tequila

45 ml (1½ fl oz) freshly squeezed lime juice

15 ml (½ fl oz) simple syrup

Classic ice cubes

1 individual bottle of Mexican beer

EQUIPMENT

Fine grater

Saucer

Jigger

Bar spoon

Thirsty, in the mood to party and yet time-poor (perhaps on your lunch break?). The Lagerita is two of your favourite drinks in one chilled, frosty package – and, somewhat stunningly, is even simpler than the Beer & Shot.

Think of the classic Margarita base (tequila, fresh lime, a little sugar syrup if you're that way inclined), a zesty, salted rim and a top of golden chilled beer and you'll have imagined the Lagerita.

1 Cut a wedge from the lime, then zest the rest with a fine grater.

2 Add the zest to a saucer and mix with some salt.

3 Squeeze out the juice from the almost-whole zested lime, then use it to moisten the rim of the glass.

4 Dip the rim in the zest and salt mix.

5 Add tequila, lime juice, simple syrup and ice to the glass and stir.

6 Top with chilled beer and drop in the lime wedge.

Kamikaze

Glass	*Serves*	*Karaoke Track*
Shot	**3**	'Teenage Suicide (Don't Do It)' by Big Fun

INGREDIENTS

45 ml (1½ fl oz) vodka

45 ml (1½ fl oz) freshly squeezed lime juice

45 ml (1½ fl oz) Cointreau or triple sec

Classic ice cubes

EQUIPMENT

Shaker

Cocktail strainer

Dive bars are generous. What they lack in frills, they make up for in atmosphere, '90s pop tunes and free shots (bartender permitting). The Kamikaze is one such drink, served in a shot glass, and is designed to be slammed rather than sipped. It is thought the Kamikaze – a mini vodka-based margarita-style drop – was created in the 1970s and is perhaps the first shooter-style cocktail. Your bartender might build yours in the glass, but shaking it with ice and straining is a low-effort improvement; this is a drink best served chilled.

1   Shake the liquid over ice until frosty, then strain into shot glasses. Slam down with two friends.

51

BARTENDER'S CHOICE

Glass	*Serves*	*Essential Karaoke Track*
Any	1	'Bennie & the Jets' by Elton John

Dive bars are magical places. The inviting flicker of neon. The smooth shine of pleather seats. The musical churn of a broken frozen Margarita machine. And the all-night, unplanned drinkathon when you end up astride the bar top singing Elton John's 'Bennie & the Jets' from the top of your lungs (or was that *27 Dresses*?). The point is that all manner of life-changing things can happen at your local dive, but only if you're open to it. So you must gladly try the dusty-looking bar snacks, play pool with the friendly lesbian couple, deliver your best Shakira impression on the karaoke mic, let the Shiba Inu half-hidden in an Ikea bag lick the Cheeto dust from your fingers and even surrender your drink choice to the bartender. Bartender's Choice is almost always going to be the best – or at least most memorable – drink you'll have that night.

LA PIOJERA

SANTIAGO, CHILE

Step inside the most raucous, stickiest-floored graffitied and loved dive bar in the Americas. La Piojera – aka The Fleahouse – in Santiago is a locals' and visitors' hotspot, the ultimate place to have simple dinner from the grill, sing along to live folk music, treat your grandmother to a Terremoto (La Piojera's earth-shatteringly strong and weirdly camp house cocktail) or simply get loud-drunk with friends. The Fleahouse is a place to let loose.

La Piojera has always been busy: it opened in 1896 and sits next to the bustling Mercado Central, giving its clientele a democratic, everyone's-welcome vibe. Inside, the sprawling interior pops with peeps of pale orange between thousands of posters, flyers and ephemera and – up out of arms' reach delightfully wonkily painted murals. It earned its nickname in 1922 when the Chilean president Arturo Alessandri Palma wanted to visit a working-class establishment,

only the bar – then known as Santiago Antiguo – was too much for him: 'You brought me to a fleahouse?' Like a wad of well-chewed gum squished under a table, the name stuck, and La Piojera formally adopted its fleapit moniker in 1981. The neighbour has changed little since opening, with an open-air market and strip bars nearby – it's not flashy.

What to order? Fight to the front of the bar and order el Terremoto, made with sweet fermented wine, pineapple ice cream and either Fernet or grenadine drizzled on top. While it has the vibe of a polite, ceramic-painting-class bachelorette party, it's a killer – and you'll probably only be served one per visit. Daytimes are for socialising, with elderly shoppers and families, but at night, a younger, more boisterous crowd descends on the fleahouse.

7-Up
7 & 7 114

A

absinthe
   La Louisiane 116
Acapulco 140
agave syrup
   Margarita 64
   Paloma 139
Aljaff, Moe 126
allspice berries
   Hot Apple Cider 98
almonds
   Glögg 100
Amaretto Sour 120
Americano 32
Angostura bitters 25
   Cuba Libre 60
   Gin, Grapefruit
     And Bitters 118
   Manhattan 50
   Martinez 76
   NYC Sour 96
   Rob Roy 111
   Whisky Sour 78
Ankrah, Douglas 90
Aperol 25
apples/apple juice
   Hot Apple Cider 98

B

bar spoons 16
bars
   The Bearded Tit (Sydney) 103
   B.Y.G. (Tokyo) 54
   Candlelight Lounge
     (New Orleans) 136
   Chez Jeannette (Paris) 41
   La Piojera (Santiago) 148
   Salty Dawg Saloon
     (Alaska) 66
   Stonewall Inn (New York) 28
   Sunny's (Redhook) 74
   Trisha's (London) 89
   Two Schmucks (Barcelona) 126
Bartender's Choice 146
The Bearded Tit (Sydney) 103

beer
   Lagerita 143
   Michelada 104
Benedictine
   La Louisiane 116
Bergonzi, Trish 89
Birnbac, Lisa 108
Bishop, Charlie 38
bitters 25
blender 15
Bloody Maria and Her Sisters 56
Bloody Mary 52
Blue Curaçao
   Yale Cocktail 108
boards 17
Boilermaker 47
Boston glasses 18
Boulevardier 80
bourbon 25
   Amaretto Sour 120
   Boulevardier 80
   NYC Sour 96
   Whisky Sour 78
Bourdain, Anthony 74
Bradsell, Dick 85
Butt, Robert 38
B.Y.G. 54

C

Campari 25
   Americano 32
   Boulevardier 80
   Ferrari 30
   Negroni 35
   Negroni Sbagliato
     With Prosecco 130
   Old Pal 128
Candlelight Lounge
   (New Orleans) 136
cardamom pods
   Glögg 100
cassis 26
   Pink Gin and Tonic 123
Cecchini, Toby 43
celery
   Bloody Maria and
     Her Sisters 56
   Bloody Mary 52
Champagne
   French75 69

Champagne flutes 18
cherries
    Acapulco 140
    Amaretto Sour 120
    La Louisiane 116
    Man About Town 94
    Manhattan 50
    Rob Roy 111
    Tequila Sunrise 134
    Whisky Sour 78
cherry liqueur
    Martinez 76
Chez Jeannette
    (Paris) 41
chilling 22
cinnamon sticks
    Glögg 100
    Hot Apple Cider 98
citrus squeezers 17
citrus vodka
    Cosmopolitan 43
citrus wedges
    Vermouth & Tonic 82
cloves
    Glögg 100
    Hot Apple Cider 98
Coca cola
    Cuba Libre 60
cocktail strainers 16
coffee
    Cold Brew Spritzer 125
    Espresso Martini 85
coffee liqueur
    Espresso Martini 85
Cointreau
    Cosmopolitan 43
    Kamikaze 144
cola
    Long Island Iced Tea 38
Cold Brew Spritzer 125
Collins glasses 21
Collins, Wayne 36
Cook, Cheryl 43
Cooke, Olivia 130
Cosmopolitan 43
Coupe glasses 18
Craddock, Harry 63, 70
cranberry juice
    Cosmopolitan 43
Cuba Libre 60
Cynar
    Man About Town 94

Daiquiri 59
Damon, Matt 32
D'Arcy, Emma 130
DeGroff, Dale 43
Dirty Martini 86
dogs 63, 132

E

egg white
    Acapulco 140
    Amaretto Sour 120
    NYC Sour 96
    Whisky Sour 78
Espresso Martini 85

F

Fernet-Branca
    Ferrari 30
Ferrari 30
French 75 69

G

Gimlet 70
gin 26
    French 75 69
    Gimlet 70
    Gin, Grapefruit And Bitters 118
    Long Island Iced Tea 38
    Martinez 76
    Negroni 35
    Negroni Bianco 36
    The Perfect Gin & Tonic 44
    Pink Gin and Tonic 123
    Tom Collins 72
    Yale Cocktail 108
Gin, Grapefruit And Bitters 118
ginger
    Glögg 100
ginger beer
    Moscow Mule 48
glasses 16, 18–21
Glögg 100
Gramercy Tavern 94

Grandison, Leona 136
grapefruit/grapefruit juice
    Acapulco 140
    Gin, Grapefruit And Bitters 118
    Greyhound 63
    Negroni Bianco 36
    Paloma 139
    The Perfect Gin & Tonic 44
    Salty Dog 132
grenadine
    Tequila Sunrise 134
Greyhound 63
Gwynne, Erskine 'Foxy' 80

Hemingway, Ernest 59
Highball glasses 19
Hot Apple Cider 98
Hurricane glasses 19

I

ice 22

J

Jägerbomb 92
Jägermeister
    Jägerbomb 92
jalapeños
    Bloody Maria and
    Her
    Sisters 56
Jessel, George 52
jiggers 15

K

Kamikaze 144
knives 17
Koppi Roasters Café 125

L

La Louisiane 116
La Piojera (Santiago) 148

Lady Gaga 74
lager
 Boilermaker 47
 Shandy 107
Lagerita 143
Larrouy, Juliette 126
Law, Jude 32
lemon soda
 Shandy 107
lemons/lemon juice
 Amaretto Sour 120
 Americano 32
 Bloody Maria and
  Her Sisters 56
 Bloody Mary 52
 Cold Brew Spritzer 125
 French 75 69
 Hot Apple Cider 98
 Long Island Iced Tea 38
 Martinez 76
 NYC Sour 96
 Old Pal 128
 Oyster Bay 113
 Tom Collins 72
 Whisky Sour 78
Lillet Blanc
 Negroni Bianco 36
limes/lime juice
 Cosmopolitan 43
 Cuba Libre 60
 Daiquiri 59
 Gimlet 70
 Greyhound 63
 Kamikaze 144
 Lagerita 143
 Margarita 64
 Michelada 104
 Moscow Mule 48
 Paloma 139
 Porn Star Martini 90
Long Island Iced Tea 38

M

MacElhone, Harry 80
Maggi sauce
 Michelada 104
Man About Town 94
Manhattan 50
maple syrup
 Hot Apple Cider 98

Margarita 64
Martin, John 48
Martinez 76
Martini glasses 19
measuring 22
Michelada 104
mixing glasses 16
Modeste, Pom 126
Morgan, John 48
Morgenthaler,
 Jeffrey 116
Moscow Mule 48
Moscow Mule glasses 19

N

Negroni 35
Negroni Bianco
 With Prosecco 130
Ng, Joy 103
Nick & Nora glasses 18
NYC Sour 96

O

O'Connor,
 John E. 86
Old Fashioned
 glasses 21
Old Pal 128
olive brine
 Dirty Martini 86
olives
 Bloody Mary 52
 Dirty Martini 86
orange bitters
 Manhattan 50
 Oyster Bay 113
orange curaçao liqueur
 Oyster Bay 113
orange liqueur 27
 Margarita 64
oranges/orange juice
 Boulevardier 80
 Ferrari 30
 Glögg 100
 Hot Apple Cider 98
 Negroni 35
 Tequila Sunrise 134
Oyster Bay 113

P

Paloma 139
passion fruit
 Porn Star Martini 90
Passoã liqueur
 Porn Star Martini 90
The Perfect Gin & Tonic 44
Petiot, Fernand 52
Peychaud's bitters
 La Louisiane 116
 Yale Cocktail 108
pineapple/pineapple juice
 Acapulco 140
Pink Gin and Tonic 123
Porn Star Martini 90
Prohibition 134
prosecco
 Negroni Sbagliato
  With Prosecco 130
 Porn Star Martini 90

R

raisins
 Glögg 100
Red Bull
 Jägerbomb 92
Rob Roy 111
ruby port
 Glögg 100
rum 26
 Acapulco 140
 Cuba Libre 60
 Daiquiri 59
 Hot Apple Cider 98
 Long Island Iced Tea 38
rye whiskey 26
 La Louisiane 116
 Man About Town 94
 Manhattan 50
 Old Pal 128

S

salt
 Lagerita 143
 Margarita 64
 Michelada 104
 Salty Dog 132

Salty Dawg Saloon (Alaska) 66
Salty Dog 132
Scarselli, Forsco 35
Scotch 26
    Oyster Bay 113
    Rob Roy 111
Seagram's 7 Crown Whiskey 114
Sex and the City 43
shakers 15
shaking 22
Shandy 107
shot glasses 21
simple syrup
    Acapulco 140
    Amaretto Sour 120
    Daiquiri 59
    Espresso Martini 85
    French 75 69
    Gimlet 70
    Lagerita 143
    Long Island Iced Tea 38
    NYC Sour 96
    Porn Star Martini 90
    Tom Collins 72
    Whisky Sour 78
Snoop Dog 70
soda water
    Americano 32
    Paloma 139
    Tom Collins 72
Sour glasses 21
spoons 16
squeezers 17
stirring 22
Stonewall Inn (New York) 28
strainers 16
sugar
    Glögg 100
Sunny's (Redhook) 74
Suze
    Negroni Bianco 36
syrup 27

T

Tabasco
    Bloody Maria and
      Her Sisters 56
    Bloody Mary 52
    Michelada 104

Tajin powder Michelada 104
The Talented Mr. Ripley 32
tequila 27
    Acapulco 140
    Bloody Maria and
      Her Sisters 56
    Lagerita 143
    Long Island Iced Tea 38
    Margarita 64
    Paloma 139
    Tequila Sunrise 134
Tequila Sunrise 134
Thomas, Jerry 76, 78
Tiki mugs 21
Tom Collins 72
tomato juice
    Bloody Maria and
      Her Sisters 56
    Bloody Mary 52
    Michelada 104
tonic water
    Cold Brew Spritzer 125
    Gin, Grapefruit And Bitters ... 118
    The Perfect Gin & Tonic 44
    Pink Gin and Tonic 123
    Vermouth & Tonic 82
triple sec 27
    Long Island Iced Tea 38
Trisha's (London) 89
'Tu Vuò' fà' L'Americano' 32
Two Schmucks (Barcelona) 126

V

vermouth 27
    Americano 32
    Boulevardier 80
    Dirty Martini 86
    La Louisiane 116
    Man About Town 94
    Manhattan 50
    Martinez 76
    Negroni 35
    Negroni Sbagliato
      With Prosecco 130
    Old Pal 128
    Oyster Bay 113
    Rob Roy 111
    Vermouth & Tonic 82
    Yale Cocktail 108

Vermouth & Tonic 82
vodka 27
    Bloody Mary 52
    Cold Brew Spritzer 125
    Dirty Martini 86
    Espresso Martini 85
    Glögg 100
    Greyhound 63
    Kamikaze 144
    Long Island Iced Tea 38
    Moscow Mule 48
    Porn Star Martini 90
    Salty Dog 132

W

Waldorf Astoria 111
whisk(e)y 27
    7 & 7 114
    Boilermaker 47
Whisky Sour 78
White, A.J. 126
wine
    Glögg 100
    NYC Sour 96
Worcestershire sauce
    Bloody Maria and
      Her Sisters 56
    Bloody Mary 52
    Michelada 104

Y

Yale Cocktail 108

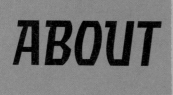

ABOUT

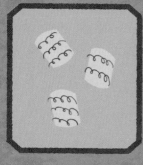

Dan Jones
is a best-selling
British writer
living and boozing
in Brooklyn.
His favourite
dive bar cocktail
is the Manhattan,
favourite snack:
the Scampi Fry.

ACKNOWLEDGEMENTS

Thanks to
Kate Pollard,
Matt Tomlinson,
Evi-O.Studio,
Jon Gartenberg,
David Deitch,
Tom McDonald,
Michael Chiang,
Tyler Wetherall
and Lotte Jones.

Published in 2023 by OH Editions,
an imprint of Welbeck Non-Fiction Ltd,
part of the Welbeck Publishing Group.
Offices in London, 20 Mortimer Street,
London, W1T 3JW, and Sydney,
Level 17, 207 Kent St, Sydney,
NSW 2000, Australia

www.welbeckpublishing.com

Design © 2023 OH Editions
Text © 2023 Dan Jones
Illustrations © 2023 Evi-O.Studio

A CIP catalogue record for this book is available
from the British Library.

ISBN 978-1-80453-098-6

Publisher: Kate Pollard
Editor: Matt Tomlinson
Art Director: Evi-O.Studio | Susan Le
Designer: Evi-O.Studio | Emi Chiba
Illustrator: Evi-O.Studio | Emi Chiba & Siena Zadro
Production: Jess Brisley
Printed and bound by Leo Paper

10 9 8 7 6 5 4 3 2 1